Assessment in the Second Language Writing Classroom

The Michigan Series on Teaching Multilingual Writers

Series Editors
Diane Belcher (Georgia State University) and
Jun Liu (University of Arizona)

Available titles in the series

Treatment of Error in Second Language Student Writing
Dana R. Ferris

Peer Response in Second Language Writing Classrooms
Jun Liu & Jette G. Hansen

Critical Academic Writing and Multilingual Students
A. Suresh Canagarajah

Controversies in Second Language Writing: Dilemmas and Decisions in Research and Instruction
Christine Pearson Casanave

Connecting Reading & Writing in Second Language Writing Instruction
Alan Hirvela

Genre and Second Language Writing
Ken Hyland

Teacher Written Commentary in Second Language Writing Classrooms
Lynn M. Goldstein

Connecting Speaking & Writing in Second Language Writing Instruction
Robert Weissberg

Technologies in the Second Language Composition Classroom
Joel Bloch

Assessment in the Second Language Writing Classroom

Deborah Crusan
Wright State University

The Michigan Series on Teaching Multilingual Writers

Ann Arbor
The University of Michigan Press
Series Editors: Diane Belcher and Jun Liu

Published in the United States of America
The University of Michigan Press
Manufactured in the United States of America

Printed on acid-free paper

ISBN-13: 978-0-472-03419-2

2013 2012 2011 2010 4 3 2 1

Library of Congress Cataloging-in-Publication Data

Crusan, Deborah.
Assessment in the second language writing classroom / Deborah Crusan.
p. cm. — (The Michigan series on teaching multilingual writers)
Includes bibliographical references and index.
ISBN 978-0-472-03419-2 (pbk. : alk. paper)
1. English language--Study and teaching—Foreign speakers. 2. Language and languages—Study and teaching. 3. Rhetoric—Study and teaching. 4. Second language acquisition. I. Title.
PE1128.A2C766 2010
808'.042076—dc22 2010021551

For Harvey, Leslie, and Lillian Grey

Series Foreword

For many teachers of second language writers, and perhaps teachers in general, assessment may seem a necessary evil: an impediment to their supportive roles as nurturers of their students' learning, a tedious and labor-intensive chore, or, still worse, an institutional or government-mandated imposition of goals and measurement tools oblivious to the learning styles and accomplishments of specific students in specific settings that their teachers know best. Yet, as Deborah Crusan makes clear in this volume, to try to ignore or distance oneself as much as possible from the "evils" of assessment can mean, at the very least, missing an opportunity to enhance classroom practice with the invaluable input that reliable and valid performance assessment data can provide. In an age when assessment is increasingly high-tech, corporate, and, some would argue, politically motivated, it may even be dangerous if those with students' interests at heart do not actively engage with writing assessment issues—dangerous for students struggling with a new language, whose futures may be determined by test scores, and dangerous for teachers as professionals, who, if content to leave assessment concerns to others, may see their decision-making power and ability to chart courses of instruction tailored to their students' needs jeopardized.

An active assessment researcher herself and experienced secondary and post-secondary classroom teacher and teacher trainer, Crusan not only makes a compelling case for becoming knowledgeable about L2 writing assessment, but offers the means to do so. Her highly accessible, thought-provoking presentation of the conceptual and practical dimensions of writing assessment, both for the classroom and on a larger scale, promises to engage readers who have previously found the technical detail of other works on assessment off-putting, as well as those who have had no previous exposure to the study of assessment at all. Crusan assumes no prior knowledge on her readers' part, but she does assume her readers can and will care about her subject; her passion for it will very likely prove to be contagious.

Diane Belcher
Georgia State University

Jun Liu
University of Arizona

Acknowledgments

My quest for justice, fairness, and individual student needs has driven me to explore the political motivation and the economic and social consequences of writing assessment, but I could never have done this alone. There are many people to thank, without whose generosity this book would not have happened.

I am indebted to former students Trisha Folck, Emily Franklin, Karen Hayes, Charis Nims, Julie Prugh, and Sharon Tjaden-Glass for generously allowing me to use their syllabi, assignments, and rubrics.

I have been helped along the way by Wright State colleagues, past and present, who have read my work, offered helpful feedback, and provided a quiet, collegial place to write: Angela Beumer-Johnson, Heidi Breuer, Erin Flanagan, Lance Greene, Lynette Jones, Doug Lantry, Peggy Lindsey, Noeleen McIlvenna, Alex McLeod, Carol Mejia-LaPerle, David Seitz, and Sarah Twill.

Writing is a solitary endeavor, but so much of what other people have taught me is present in this book. Particularly, I would like to thank very important teachers in my life. Karen E. Johnson, my former advisor, taught me so many important notions, particularly the value of a reflective pedagogy and the all-important answer, "It depends!" Patrick Shannon encouraged me to think critically, question everything, and view assessment as a politically charged issue. Grant Henning, my language testing professor, showed me that there are many stakeholders in assessment, all with valid positions.

Colleagues in the field of second language writing, especially Dana Ferris, read drafts and offered valuable suggestions, which led to significant improvements in the manuscript.

When I was unable to teach in the writing classroom, talks with Margi Wald reminded me of the reality of the second language writing teacher. My debt to distant colleagues is evidenced in the book's reference list, but I want to specifically mention a few leaders in the field of second language writing, assessment, and writing assessment who have especially inspired me and from whom I have learned so much: Liz Hamp-Lyons, Richard Haswell, Brian Huot, Lorraine Valdez-Pierce, and Edward M. White.

I owe a deep debt of gratitude to my dear friend Roger Frantz for his intelligent comments from a language testing perspective, for his belief in my ability to write this book, and for his constant support.

I thank my family for their support and belief in me—Mom (Lillian), Anne, Fred Anthony, Kathleen, Mark, Nicholas, John, and Lillian Grey. In particular, I am grateful to my daughter, Leslie. As she has always done, she offered me tremendous support and never doubted—even when I did—that her mom could finish this project.

I am incredibly appreciative of series editors Diane Belcher and Jun Liu who flattered me with the invitation to write this book and waited patiently for the final product. Kelly Sippell, Executive Acquisitions Editor at the University of Michigan Press, tirelessly supported me, answered my many questions, and offered continual encouragement. Hanging in there with me has meant more than she knows.

Finally, my heartfelt appreciation goes to Harvey Bank, chief editor, tireless reader, and life partner, who spent countless hours on my manuscript, consistently posing hard questions about assessment from an outsider's perspective. A scientist, he taught me the value of careful and intense research and became quite well versed in assessment as we worked together.

The writing of this book was supported in part by a Faculty Development Leave from Wright State University, Dayton, Ohio.

Contents

Introduction 1

Why This Book? 1

What's in This Book? 3

1. Historical and Theoretical Contexts of Second Language Writing Assessment 5

Why Assessment Matters 8

Assessment: Every Teacher's Job 10

How Is Writing Ability Defined? 13

Good Assessment Defined 14

The Importance of Historical Perspective for L2 Writing Teachers 17

A Brief History of Writing Assessment 19

A History of the Field 25

The Influence of Science and Measurement on L2 Writing Assessment 27

Suggestions for Teachers 30

Suggestions for Further Reading 30

2. An Overview of the Tools of Writing Assessment 31

Purposes for Assessing Writing 32

Rules of Writing Assessment 33

Standards 34

Objectives 38

Reliability 39

Validity 41

Practicality 42

Washback 42

Rubrics 43

Writing Assignments 50

Suggestions for Teachers 55

3. Designing Assignments and Rubrics **56**
Personal Experience as a Student 57
Personal Experience as a Teacher 58
Considerations in Designing Assessments 59
Designing Assignment/Assessment Tasks for the Classroom 64
Timed Essays and Prompt Development 64
Criteria Generation 70
Rubric Creation 72
Peer Review and Its Place in Writing Assessment 77
Portfolio Assessment 79
Suggestions for Teachers 86

4. Biases in Writing Assessment: What Are They and What Can We Do about Them? **87**
Teacher Bias 89
Teachers' (Assessors') Personality Types 91
Bias Regarding Pedagogy 92
Bias toward Grammar Correctness 98
Peer Bias 104
Administrative Bias 107
Political Bias 111
Suggestions for Teachers 113
Suggestions for Further Reading 114

5. Large-Scale Writing Assessment and Its Influences on L2 Writing **115**
An Overview of Large-Scale Writing Tests: Product and Purpose 116
Advantages and Disadvantages of Standardized Tests of Writing 124
The Politics and Business of Assessment 129
The Effect of NCLB Legislation on the L2 Writer 131
Strategies for Making Large-Scale Writing Assessment Work 133
Suggestions for Teachers 136
Suggestions for Further Reading 136

6. Innovative Technology in the L2 Writing Classroom **137**

Technology in the Classroom 137

Using Synchronous and Asynchronous Technology for Assessing Writing 138

The Impact of Technology on L2 Writing Assessment 143

ODSP 144

The Dark Side of the Internet: Paper Mills 146

Combating Internet Plagiarism 147

Outsourcing of Grading 148

Suggestions for Teachers 154

7. Looking Beyond: What Can We Expect of Writing Assessment in the Future? The Machine Scoring of Essays **156**

Machine Scoring of Essays Defined 157

Origins of the Machine Scoring of Essays 161

Major Purveyors of Machine Scoring 164

A Closer Look: MY Access! 167

Writing as Meaning Making 171

Positive Views 172

Negative Views 173

Professional Claims 174

Truth and Consequences 176

Suggestions for Teachers 179

Suggestions for Further Reading 179

Epilogue: Where Do We Go from Here? **180**

ELL Population in the United States 180

Teacher Training 181

The Uses of Technology for Assessment 182

Large-Scale Assessment/Accountability 184

Final Thoughts 185

Appendix 1 **186**

References **189**

Index **206**

Introduction

Why This Book?

Assessment in the Second Language Writing Classroom is a teacher-friendly and prospective teacher–friendly book, uncomplicated by the language of statistics. The book was written for those who teach and assess second language writing in several different contexts: the IEP, the developmental writing classroom, and the sheltered composition classroom. Teachers who experience a mixed population or teach cross-cultural composition will also find the book a valuable resource.

Assessment is one of the most important of the many tasks for which teachers are responsible. Learning to do good, honest, and criteria-based assessment is crucial for all teachers, especially writing teachers. Although several books thoroughly cover the theoretical aspects of writing assessment (Huot, 2002; Weigle, 2002; White, 1998, 2007), none concentrate as heavily on the practical classroom aspects of writing assessment as this book does. Further, no book has as yet included an in-depth examination of the machine scoring of writing and its effects on second language writers.

This book also reflects my interest in the assessment of second language (L2) writing, which began very early in my teaching career at a small community college in western Pennsylvania. It was then that I faced the stark realization of the consequences of assessment when, as a brand new (and powerless) adjunct, my students questioned me about why they had been placed in the developmental English class I was teaching. I promised these students that I would find out why they had been placed in my class rather than in the for-credit class they thought they should be taking. When I was told that their placement was based on their scores on a multiple choice grammar test rather than actual writing, I attempted to dispute what I perceived an injustice with the powers that be. I quickly realized that I did not know enough about the placement and assessment system to function as an effective advocate for my students. From that point on, I became a self-appointed crusader for fairness in assessment in general and writing assessment in particular. I was inspired to write this book because I was moved by the plight of my students who were/are marginalized by assessment procedures and wanted to share my understanding of this increasingly complicated and politicized field.

One thing I have learned is that it is very important to understand why we do what we do (Johnson, 1999). When we profoundly reflect on our practices, we often realize why we do what we do and how to change if change is warranted. We can and should improve our practices. Embedded in every chapter of this book is the notion of teacher reflection and improvement of pedagogy.

I also wanted to write this book because I believe that many teachers are unprepared to systematically establish and use criteria to assess writing. Teachers are responsible for assessment as well as ethics in assessment and are certainly stakeholders in assessment (Hamp-Lyons, 2000). However, many seem unprepared to accept this responsibility, which is certainly troubling (Crusan, 2006). In my experience, many new teachers of writing are naïve about assessment, and I include myself. I remember how unprepared I was the first time I taught writing. My first assignment established no criteria by which I would fairly assess what my students had written. Worse yet, I was not sure where I might find help. I quickly realized that while I had my degree and understood different pedagogical approaches, I had little expertise in the teaching of writing and still less in writing assessment. My teacher preparation courses had failed me, especially the testing and measurements course in which the professor had spent nearly the entire semester teaching us to write multiple choice questions. I remembered my feelings of helplessness and a little shame, and when I was given the responsibility of preparing teachers for the classroom, I vowed that they would not be as naïve, helpless, or ashamed as I had been.

I believe that teachers need a strong historical and theoretical background in writing assessment and a familiarity with the seminal publications in the field. They need to know the politics involved in assessment, to be familiar with the purposes for writing assessment—admission, placement, in class, and exit. They should be comfortable with the tools of writing assessment (rubrics, scoring guides, criteria)—among them holistic, analytic, primary trait, and multiple trait—and be able to create their own rubrics and to clearly articulate criteria for assignments. Finally, teachers should be well-informed test consumers: they need to know the assumptions inherent in standardized testing; they need to understand the proper use of such tests; and they need to be able to intelligently articulate their objections to the misuse of these tests. I am hopeful that readers will benefit from the treatment of those issues within these pages.

What's in This Book?

Throughout the book, I provide not only practical information about how to do assessment, but I also challenge the ways teachers think about writing assessment and, possibly, assessment in general. To be critical of assessment—to understand the appropriate uses of standardized tests, and the political, economic, and sociological ramifications of tests—helps teachers protect their students from the onslaught of perhaps well-intentioned, but possibly detrimental, tests. This book offers no quick-fix solutions because assessing writing is far from easy, but when it is done well, it can produce better teachers and better writers.

Assessment in the Second Language Writing Classroom has seven chapters and an epilogue. The first chapter discusses the history and theory relevant to writing assessment in general and L2 writing assessment specifically. This chapter serves as a foundation for the rest of the book, helping readers understand the reasons why we assess writing the way we do. Although I freely admit a basic bias about assessment—I come to assessment from a teaching perspective—I recognize the need for a strong foundation upon which to base our practices.

Chapter 2 discusses the ABCs of assessment, delving into such issues as standards, objectives, reliability, validity, washback or impact, rubrics, and writing assignments for different purposes of assessing writing; it also provides examples of various assignments, rubrics, and criteria from a variety of teachers and contexts. Chapter 3 provides instructions for creating assignments, feedback tools, and rubrics necessary for good writing assessment. The fourth chapter discusses a variety of biases inherent in writing assessment, asking readers to consider their own prejudices and recognizing ways to combat them. Chapter 5 discusses the major standardized tests that are used to assess second language writing and the political and ethical issues at play. Chapter 6 looks specifically at the use of technology to provide feedback and to formatively and summatively assess student writing. It further explores the synchronous and asynchronous tools that students use for writing and that teachers find valuable in providing feedback to their students. Further, the chapter questions our fascination with the essay and discusses other ways to prepare our students for their futures.

Particularly relevant to the future is the topic of machine scoring of essays; Chapter 7 provides one philosophical and ethical perspective regarding the use of such programs. The Epilogue considers the future of writing assessment and suggests where we go next in writing assessment and the issues that need to be considered.

It is my fervent hope that through this book, readers will understand that "all assessment practices are political" (Hamp-Lyons, 2001, p. 117). It is vitally important that teachers recognize that when they undertake assessment, they are undertaking an important political process.

Chapter 1

Historical and Theoretical Contexts of Second Language Writing Assessment

We should not look back unless it is to derive useful lessons from past errors and for the purpose of profiting by dearly bought experience.

—George Washington

Assessing student writing is quite possibly one of the most time-consuming (and) scary but most significant things teachers do. It is generally considered one of the biggest problems confronting writing instructors (both English and English as a Second Language) and composition program administrators today because assessing writing requires patience, a great deal of conscious preparation of assignments and criteria, and painstaking decision-making about student writing. Teachers at every level and in every context are gradually realizing how important the act of assessment is, an act that teachers perform again and again. And yet, many of us still reject any association with assessment, possibly because of its association with testing, psychometrics, and the standardized testing industry. The importance of responsible assessment practices cannot be underestimated, however, because assessment measures influence critical decisions. Like it or not, tests determine whether a student will pass on to another grade or level or whether a student will graduate (as in No Child Left Behind). Furthermore, in colleges and universities, tests control placement into composition classes, an act laden with pedagogical, ethical, political, psychometric, and financial implications. Bullock (1991) reminds us: "Any project to assess individual students' writing abilities, over time or in a single instance, is fraught with philosophical, ethical, and methodological peril" (p. 195). Bullock's words serve as a reminder that evaluation is far from neutral; tests have become a dominant force impacting both individuals and society.

Tests shape curricula and define what is and is not worth teaching and knowing. Evidence that federally mandated tests are changing what our children learn in school is all around us. Seldom does a day go by without a newspaper article or a radio or television news story about testing in our public schools and its effects on schools, teachers, and students. Simply put, assessment and teachers have much in common: both shape the lives of students.

Nevertheless, many teachers believe that assessment is not within their circle of influence, that someone outside the classroom should take on responsibility for it (usually testing organizations in charge of large-scale assessments). However, if teachers accept responsibility for their students and are invested in the belief that students should be fairly evaluated, then they must be involved with the assessment of their students (Hamp-Lyons, 2003). Further, if teachers give up control of assessment, someone outside their classrooms will control assessment. For instance, at my institution, we face a consistent barrage of requests from our testing services department inviting the Program in ESL to adopt online writing placement services. While the adoption of such outside assessment might make our jobs easier, the consequences of adopting these tests for placement would be deleterious for many reasons and on multiple levels. One consequence of adopting assessment measures developed outside local contexts revolves around what students need to know or be able to do in the particular context. Might students at one institution need to know something or be able to do something a bit different from students at another institution? Might the definitions of good writing or the very reasons for writing differ from institution to institution and from department to department? Moreover, outside assessment causes teachers to teach to that standardized measurement at the expense of creativity, teacher and student interest, and productive class time, sometimes sacrificing depth of understanding for surface knowledge of facts. A teacher who relinquishes control of assessment risks losing control of much of what goes on within her classroom.

Also, once institutions lose control of assessment, regaining that control is difficult, if not impossible (Haswell & Wyche-Smith, 1994), and the resulting assessments may very well be at odds with some of the teachers' pedagogical philosophies. Most important, teachers need to be cognizant that curriculum and evaluation are inextricably connected and that curriculum should guide assessment; assessment should never set the curriculum (Shannon, 2001; Shohamy, 2001). Examples of this narrowing of curriculum can be found everywhere. Addressing the 2005 incorporation of an essay test into the SAT®, Diane Fettrow, Broward County (Miami, FL) Public Schools Language Arts Curriculum Specialist for Secondary Schools, claims, "Teachers have narrowed their instruction to the tests that are given instead of looking at the whole spectrum of writing. Maybe some teachers have given up the writing of poetry in class because they have to prepare students for a test, and I'm not happy with that" (Cole, 2005, p. 1).

"More than many issues within the field of composition studies, writing assessment evokes strong passions" (Conference on College Composition and Communication [CCCC] Committee on Assessment, 1995, p. 430). These strong feelings are often the result of how writing ability is defined—one's *definition* of writing ability drives the means by which one *assesses* writing ability. As might be expected, writing assessment is often considered contentious and problematic. Some problems can be attributed to "the lack of a firm theoretical base" (Huot, 1990, p. 258), some with the assessment instruments used, some with the manner of scoring, and others with the entire process.

As a field, we have difficulty agreeing on and articulating what good writing is and, consequently, have difficulty agreeing on ways to assess it. Belanoff (1991) claims, "Our profession has no agreed upon definition of proficiency and certainly, as a consequence, no agreed upon definitions for proficiencies at various levels of schooling" (p. 58). Leki (1995) concurs and maintains that we make assumptions about what good writing is and assume that everyone else, including our students, knows what our assumptions are. She reminds us that good writing is highly contextualized and that we need to "develop awareness of what other faculty on our campuses are assuming about writing" (p. 45) to make certain that our students are aware of the spectrum of faculty expectations regarding writing. This is no small task.

Chaper 1 discusses why writing assessment matters, argues that assessment, regardless of its contentious and often disconcerting nature, is every teacher's job, defines writing ability and good writing assessment, discusses the relationship between writing ability and the choice of writing assessment method, demonstrating their interdependence, and presents a brief history of writing assessment, situated mostly in the United States, examining its deep relationship to the history of composition, both L1 and L2.

By doing these things, I locate assessment theories and practices in teaching environments, thus providing the background information for a theoretical framework. As a result, teachers will be able to articulate what they mean by writing assessment and discuss more confidently the principles that drive writing assessment; moreover, teachers will be able to examine and possibly transform their own writing assessment beliefs and practices.

Why Assessment Matters

Assessment is everywhere. We perform assessments all the time. We make assessments (or judgments) about hundreds of things, big and small, every day—the tomatoes at the farmer's market, our friend's new haircut, the weather and how it might affect our weekend plans, the job of our football coach, the fabric for a new sofa, the latest technology, what we will include in a class we're planning. We are often quick and many times relentless in our decision-making. It's in our nature. Assessment assists us in making all kinds of decisions, helps us grow intellectually and socially, and maybe saves our lives.

Writing is both important and complex. Through writing, we discern meaning. The struggle to put words on paper (or on the blank computer screen) can clarify our thoughts like no other process can, leading to increased complexity of thought. Regarding writing as a process, its messiness and complexity, Murray (1980) notably claimed that writing is *rewriting*. And this is where writing assessment matters. Without the ability to assess writing, to notice good writing, to understand what we are saying and what we are meaning to say, we, as teachers and as writers, sacrifice a valuable avenue of communication.

Writers rarely move through a piece of writing in any linear fashion. Generally, writers shuffle back and forth, engaged in a process that features phases of planning, revising, reflection, drafting, and researching. Writers need to become critical assessors of their own writing; as they shuffle back and forth through the various phases of writing, they are assessing what they have written. For those struggling with language, writing can promote fluency. Through assessment, most writers can learn to be more careful evaluators of their own writing as well as the writing of others. This is a necessary skill because many times in life we will be asked for our input and ideas in writing.

Weigle (2007) reminds us that writing assessment is one of the most fundamental duties of a writing teacher. Like me, she is passionate about adequate preparation of writing teachers "to construct, administer, score, and communicate the results of valid and reliable classroom tests" (p. 195). She also believes that teachers need to know about "the uses and misuses of large-scale assessments" (p. 195) to become effective supporters of their students when faced with mandatory assessments. Hamp-Lyons (2002) reminds us that writing assessment matters because it remains unexamined, that the written word remains the principle means of communication, and "that access to written language, and to writing in English in particular, remains a 'good' that greatly influences access to many, even, most, other 'goods' in the twenty-first century world. When writing is assessed, that which is assessed is less well-understood than many other constructs. The questions: What is good writing? How do we know? According to whom? and similar ones, remain intriguing because they remain unresolved" (p. 5). Hamp-Lyons raises critically important questions. I would be overconfident, perhaps arrogant, if I were to claim that I could answer them; however, I will attempt to address them in a variety of contexts. In this way, I hope to raise the awareness of second language writing teachers to the importance of the act of assessment, an act they perform every time they walk into a classroom, create an assignment, or talk to students about their writing.

Assessment: Every Teacher's Job

Writing assessment is fundamental to the work of writing teachers. Its many applications and its ubiquitous nature make it impossible to ignore. Moreover, writing assessment is incredibly complex. Perhaps that is why many teachers approach writing assessment with more than a little consternation, but, ironically, teachers who teach writing (generally) also *assess* writing. Some teachers shrink from writing assessment (Hamp-Lyons, 2003; Weigle, 2007), claiming a complexity beyond their understanding coupled with a fundamental distaste for statistics and/or confusion about what constitutes good assessment. Many other writing teachers often either have an aversion to writing assessment (Yancey, 1999; Weigle, 2007) or do not recognize writing assessment as a fundamental component of a teacher's responsibility (Hamp-Lyons, 2003). Therefore, they may not be systematic in their approach to assessment and quite possibly avoid assessment activities or carry out assessment without reflection. Teachers sometimes view writing assessment as villainous (Yancey, 1999), especially when events linked to assessment occur outside the classroom (e.g., the abolition of basic writing programs or mandated large-scale assessment of writing for placement). There is irony in this situation. If teachers are not involved in and do not control the forms of assessments used by their institutions, the institutions will control assessment. Even worse, some factions external to the institution with little or no vested interest in the institution or knowledge of the kinds of assessment that would benefit the specific population of students enrolled at that institution, overtly or covertly, assume control over assessment. Despite their trepidation, it is vital that teachers learn about writing assessment and become involved in the design, implementation, and politics of writing assessment at their institutions. If teachers are not involved in assessment, the loss of control will eventually seep into the classroom, affecting the kinds of assessments (and, invariably, the curriculum) teachers use; unfortunately, in many cases, it already has.

Haswell and Wysche-Smith (1994) contend that composition faculty have often found themselves ancillary to the political reform movements promoting assessment within their own institutions. "They blink an eye, and suddenly some victor is nailing a manifesto right on their classroom door directly affecting their programs and the lives of their students. The only recourse seems frustrated acceptance or angry protest" (p. 221). Much of this usurpation of power regarding assessment can be attributed to the vacuum created in the field of composition by faculty who have been slow to embrace writing assessment as an integral part of their job. White (1994) admonishes that faculty should be strong advocates for retaining control of assessment decisions such as placement of incoming freshman students into their composition classes. Faculty who teach composition are in a better position to accurately evaluate what is expected of their students than anyone outside the teaching community. White (2001) cautions us: "Once we are evaluated as unable to fulfill our roles, no one in a position of power need take seriously our claims, and our discipline becomes easy to dismiss as an expensive frill" (p. 306). Thus, despite many writing teachers' natural distaste for and anxiety about assessment, teachers must be involved in assessment at every level, from the smallest informal classroom assessments to the largest institution-wide assessments.

Assessment specialists and writing assessment specialists (Bachman and Palmer, 1996; Broad, 2003; CCCC Committee on Assessment, 1995; Crusan, 2002a, 2002b, 2006; Hamp-Lyons, 1996, 2000, 2003; Haswell and Wyche-Smith, 1994; Huot, 2002; Lynne, 2004; Weigle, 2002; White, 1994, 1996a, 2001; Wolcott & Legg, 1998; Yancey, 1999) call for writing teachers and writing program administrators (WPAs) to incorporate writing assessment as an integral part of their jobs. Like Huot, (2002) they believe writing assessment is "inextricably linked to its practice" (p. 165) and to the teaching of writing, for responsibly teaching writing requires consistent engagement in the practice of writing assessment. Further, writing assessment must be "site-based and locally controlled" (Huot, 2002, p. 19). Huot posits that those who *teach* writing should *create* writing assessment tools; further, he contends that, since every context is different, what works as assessment in one context may either not work or not work as well in another. With assessment, one size does not fit all (Gallagher, 2007; McNeil, 2000; Shannon, 2007). Hence, teachers and WPAs should be involved in the creation of contextualized assessments—assuring that each assessment is a good fit for the students they will be testing.

The concept of localized assessment allows stakeholders to make a very strong case for involvement of local faculty in *any* assessment at their institutions. Huot argues, too, for diligence on the part of teachers lest bureaucracy wrest assessment from our hands. However, even at our most diligent, we are constantly at risk of losing control over assessment, an act that has critical implications for teachers. When assessment is mandated by someone or some entity other than teachers, whether it is the type of assessment used or how often students are assessed, it is usually through means unrelated to curriculum, with the resultant tail wagging the dog phenomenon—test-driven curriculum—rather than the opposite, and far more robust, curriculum-driven assessment.

How Is Writing Ability Defined?

As mentioned previously, one's definition of writing ability deeply affects one's notion of writing assessment. When asked for a definition, I often respond: "It depends" (Johnson, 1999, p. 1). Or maybe more pointedly: It depends on whom you ask. In the past few years, the U.S. government has been orchestrating and mandating assessment practices, pedagogy, and research for its K–12 institutions. Behind this mandate is the quest for quantifiable standardized results—improvement in student scores—that politicians can then point to as achievement. Unfortunately, such an approach may be naïve at best and potentially dangerous for students with differing abilities or diverse understandings of Western definitions of good writing. Still further, bureaucracies are attempting to impose their often-narrow definition of writing ability, and consequently writing assessment, on teachers: "WPAs often wrestle with issues relating to institutionalized definitions of 'good' writing and a one-size-fits-all mentality toward assessment; for example, institutions viewing writing and the writer as static might turn to evaluation that standardizes writing" (Crusan, 2006, p. 205). When an institution defines writing ability differently from the teachers' definition, its goals will differ from those of teachers (for more on good writing, see Chapter 4).

To most writing teachers in the United States, the definition of writing ability includes a reference to writing as a means of learning and making meaning. Further, the definition will include the ability to judge credibility of sources, argue effectively, evaluate arguments, understand and convey complex information, and systematically develop ideas. And teachers derive their assessments of the writing their students do based on their definition of writing ability. Outside the composition community, institutional and/or bureaucratic definitions of writing ability often differ substantially. (These often extend to faculty in other disciplines.) For example, institutions (and even some teachers) that define writing ability solely as mastery of conventions such as spelling, punctuation, and capitalization or as language use—agreement, tense, number, and word order—often administer tests measuring only this small subset of easily measured (and easily scored) features in the larger domain of writing ability. If institutions define writing ability as correctness of final written product rather than the nonlinear, recursive process through which a writer passes when she writes, they are likely to assess writing indirectly (measuring writing ability using grammar, vocabulary, or error detection tests). Likewise, if their definition focuses on accuracy and final product, they are correct to assess writing ability indirectly, for the assessment would certainly be valid; that is, the assessment is testing what it purports to test—the subskills of language. While indirect assessment fell into disfavor for some years (Hamp-Lyons, 2003), this method of assessment, particularly for placement, is currently enjoying a resurgence. However, whether such indirect assessment correlates meaningfully with students' ability to write coherent and effective essays is a separate but critical question.

Good Assessment Defined

Writing assessment, like all assessment, wields power, occupying a central place at the heart of educational reform, a movement brought about by dissatisfaction with traditional testing practices coupled with evolving ideas and attitudes about assessment (Wolcott & Legg, 1998). Yancey (1999) explains, "Writing assessment . . . is rhetorical: positioned as shaper of students and as a means of understanding the effects of such shaping" (p. 498). Yancey's words highlight the fundamental importance of writing assessment, a task intimately connected to the teaching of writing.

What constitutes good assessment? Again, it depends. The answers, often awash in controversy, differ depending on perspective. White (1996a) clearly demonstrates the wide gap between faculty and institutional governing bodies. White contends that test developers and administrators find these characteristics essential:

- Assessment that produces scores quickly and cheaply.
- Assessment that reduces the complexity of writing and the teaching of writing but allows for data collected to imply complex measurement.
- Assessment that heavily weighs surface features of writing and dialect features of edited American English.
- Assessment that leads to the sorting of students according to existing social patterns.
- Assessment whose meaning depends heavily on statistical explanations of sufficient complexity to invite [unintentional] misuse of scores. (p. 20) (addition mine)

Not surprisingly, these features differ dramatically from those considered important by the majority of writing teachers:

- Assessment that supports teachers' work or at least does not deny its importance.
- Assessment that recognizes the complexity of writing and of the teaching of writing.
- Assessment that respects teachers as professionals and their students as individuals.
- Assessment that will not be misused to provide simple, damaging, and misleading information. (White, 1996a, p. 14)

These characteristics, albeit perhaps a bit simplistic and polarized, serve to contrast the value systems of measurement specialists with those of teachers and articulate basic theoretical and philosophical differences. From the vantage point of teachers, practice defines assessment; from the vantage point of measurement specialists, assessment defines practice. The role standardized testing plays at the college and university level and in the K–12 arena under the auspices of No Child Left

Behind (NCLB), quite poignantly illustrates the deep divide in assessment between classroom teachers and test developers.

Writing assessment scholars continue their quest for a theory-driven definition and practice of writing assessment. Broad (2003) advocates a humanistically constructed evaluation, centered on the student, in opposition to the evaluation promoted by the measurement community, which is centered on the test. Lynne (2004) also advocates a student-centered position and argues against specialized jargon (e.g., two-factor ANOVA or cumulative distribution function) used by the measurement community. Specifically, she believes terms used to explain assessment practices "come from educational measurement theory and carry the baggage of an objectivist paradigm" (p. 3). She questions the adoption of the terms *reliability* and *validity,* which she finds so often narrowly defined, and refers to them as leftover constructs from 20th century positivism. While reliability and validity have a place in writing assessment, Lynne calls for the adoption of new terms, not weighed down by past technical usage. She offers in their place the relatively unencumbered terms *meaningful* and *ethical* (p. 116). Lynne sees statistical terms and the positivist notions they accommodate as completely mismatched with what writing teachers have discovered about how we learn to write. Particularly, positivism leans toward a snapshot approach, measuring ability in isolation; unfortunately, a snapshot can show only a part of the whole process. In other words, since any writing is a recursive process—writers compose, revise, edit—it is difficult to look at one instance of a writer's work and definitively assess that writer's ability.

Along those same lines, Hamp-Lyons (2003) argues for an approach to writing assessment that takes into account the learner and the learner's contexts, both prior and present. She, like others (see also Huot, 2002; Weigle, 2002; Yancey, 1999), views assessment in terms of reliability and validity, but these assessment specialists see these two concepts in terms more connected with Lynne's construct. These two concepts—reliability and validity—are often at the forefront of writing assessment. *Reliability* refers to the consistency of an instrument—in this case, similar means, medians, and modes for the distribution of scores of a writing test—over repeated uses under the same conditions. *Validity* refers to the instrument measuring what it claims to measure and the results obtained accurately reflecting the construct being measured. Validity measurement can be tricky, and quite possibly easily manipulated, for at a fundamental level, its measurement is deeply enmeshed with the test developer's definition of writing ability. For example, if writing ability equals mastery of language conventions, then a valid test might be an error recognition test. Many writing teachers have a different perspective; they believe that locating writing assessment in *practice* enhances its validity (Yancey, 1999). (See Chapter 3 for more about reliability and validity.)

Collectively, these scholars define assessment as a rhetorical act (Yancey, 1999). They consider assessment an integral part of every teacher's domain. Further, it is clear that there are differences in the definitions of what good writing looks like and, consequently, what good writing assessment entails. Further, while generalizations can be made regarding the way writing programs assess the writing their students do, it is important to remember that program philosophies and practices differ. Again, one size does not fit all.

The Importance of Historical Perspective for L2 Writing Teachers

An understanding of the past is fundamental to an understanding of the present. Such study grounds us theoretically (Huot, 2002; Matsuda, 2003b). Matsuda (2003b) claims, "Without knowing the context in which certain theories or pedagogical strategies developed, we will not be able to apply them or modify them in other contexts or in light of new theoretical insights" (p. 15). Further, the question really isn't *whether* teachers need to understand the theoretical and the historical, but rather *how much* they need to understand. White (2003) asks: "What is the minimum amount of theory and history necessary for responsible teaching of writing?" White believes that those who teach composition need to know at least some of the history of the field in order to avoid seductive traps such as "giving grammar drills or spelling bees, thinking they are teaching writing" (White, 2003). In other words, a knowledge of history provides the context for what has been done in the past, and how it worked and provides us with a valuable tool to determine whether or not we should repeat the same strategy.

Knowing the history of any subject decreases the probability of repetition of mistakes and grounds us in the theory of our subject. Without such contextual understanding, it is extremely difficult for teachers to make good decisions about writing assessment. Hamp-Lyons (2003) reminds us of important situations writing teachers face when they require background knowledge. Those situations include "when they plan writing tests for their own students, take part in a school-wide writing assessment, participate in decisions about what writing test to use for a specific purpose, or talk to parents about the meaning and implications of tests their children are taking" (p. 162). Teachers need considerable, very specific information about the strengths and weaknesses of available options for writing assessment to make educated decisions about this very essential component in the teaching of writing.

Acquiring historical and theoretical information is sometimes painful. Particularly among new graduate students, the term *theory* strikes some hearts with fear and trepidation. In part, these students feel distanced, perhaps even marginalized, by traditional academic prose. They question the need for understanding theory, seeing it as a group of abstract notions, having little to do with them or their teaching. However, writing assessment scholars (Huot, 2002; Weigle, 2002; White, 1995) remind us that the ways in which we assess our students clearly reflect our theoretical stance. In fact, White, Lutz, and Kamusikiri (1996) remind us: "Assessment defines goals and expresses values more clearly than do any number of mission statements" (p. 9). Objectively or subjectively, we base everything we do on a theory—a principle, a philosophy, a value, the way we believe—and this stance is clearly visible in our pedagogy.

One of the primary responsibilities of teacher educators is to demonstrate and model for their students what it means to practice from a theoretical stance. Again, what we *do* (with regard to assessment) exemplifies our theoretical stance much more than what we *say*. We need to be cognizant of assessment theory and history and the ways in which we represent them in our pedagogy. Further, it is important to note that, although the history that follows is decidedly L1-centric, it elucidates our assessment practices in second language writing as well.

A Brief History of Writing Assessment

The history of writing assessment is inexorably entangled with the history of composition. Further, L2 histories, both of writing and of writing assessment, deeply interconnect with histories of their L1 counterpart. In these histories, various forces push and pull from many directions. As the focus of composition teaching changed over time, evolving and moving from one model of instruction to another (i.e., from current-traditional models to process models), assessment followed suit. Many scholars (Broad, 2003; Elliot, 2005; Elliot, Plata, & Zelhart, 1990; Hamp-Lyons, 2001, 2002, 2003; Huot, 2002; Lindemann, 2001; Lynne, 2004; White, 1995, 2001; Yancey, 1999) have told the story of writing assessment, each from his or her own unique perspective (e.g., L1 or L2) and starting point.

Perhaps the most interesting and compelling metaphor used to view the history of writing assessment is Yancey's (1999) wave, oscillating from one mode of assessment to another. In her history, Yancey chronicles the *objective wave* (1950–1970), the *holistic wave* (1970–1986), and the *portfolio and program assessment wave* (1986–present). An example of this wave metaphor: principally for large-scale assessment (and especially for placement into community college and university composition classes), many institutions, having used faculty-read and rated essays in the past, are once again embracing indirect (read multiple choice) computer-based, often online writing assessment. These methods purport to save time and money, a notion especially championed by administrators struggling to control their budgets. Still other programs have reverted to the use of a standardized test score such as the SAT® or ACT® verbal score, using an actual writing sample only when students challenge their placement. The objective wave seems to have swept back into fashion.

Hamp-Lyons (2001) divides her writing assessment history into four generations. She traces the first three generations—*direct* (essays), *indirect* (multiple choice), and *portfolio* assessment—and situates the emerging fourth generation of writing assessment in both the *humanistic* and the *technological*. She believes an acknowledgment of the political nature of assessment will be inherent in the fourth generation and makes a compelling case for shared responsibility of the consequences of assessment.

As will soon become evident, Yancey's waves and Hamp-Lyons' generations of writing assessment are evident throughout writing assessment's past. Historically, writing assessment has vacillated from oral recitation to direct assessment via written exams to psychometrically driven "objective" tests. The cycle has been repeated many times; we have abandoned methods—does anyone currently assess writing orally?—and reinvented methods, sometimes more than once.

Essay testing (testing writing with writing) can be traced back thousands of years to the Chou period (1111–771 BCE) when the Chinese conducted "assessment *through* writing rather than assessment *of* writing" (Hamp-Lyons, 2002, p. 6). In 470 BCE, rhetoricians such as Gorgias, Socrates, Isocrates, Plato, and Aristotle taught rhetoric with little attention to form and were unconcerned about assessment—perhaps they were unconcerned about *correctness* in particular and more interested in message (Lindemann, 2001). In the late 1500s in Europe, the Jesuits used written tests; since literacy was the exclusive privilege of nobility and the clergy, the use of written examinations served as a means of social control. From the Middle Ages to the 19th century, the mode of assessment fluctuated to oral assessment. Soon, however, oral assessment was dismissed as written examinations came into vogue.

In the late 19th century, Harvard University had a major impact on the direction of composition teaching (and by association, writing assessment) in the United States (Newkirk, 1994). At that time, Harvard's perspective shifted in favor of "dispassionate scientific systemization" (Elliot, 2005, p. 9). On its first entrance exam, Harvard failed 157 out of 316 students mostly because of errors in mechanics: spelling, lack of familiarity with material, punctuation errors, incorrect capitalization, gross grammatical errors, and obscure writing style (Elliot, 2005). Harvard's equating of accuracy with intelligence led to an American cultural preoccupation with linguistic correctness (Connors, 1990) and the first American college literacy crisis. At the forefront of the crusade for correctness were British rhetoricians Campbell, Blair, Whately, and others who focused on current-traditional rhetoric, a positivistic and inductive theory of composition with a concentration on correctness and ideological homogenization (Berlin, 1987).

In 1900, a group seeking "uniformity" (Elliot, 2005, p. 341) of college admission requirements created the College Entrance Examination Board (CEEB), which launched the first systematic testing program in the United States. With this single event, "the accountability movement in education had been concretized" (Elliot, 2005, p. 341). The examination board believed that its work in and emphasis on testing would cause secondary schools to focus more attention on English, history, and the social sciences and enforce standards of attainment (Elliot, 2005, p. 29). Further, board members believed their plan for rating students' writing was fair, and that they had arrived at a common standard of assessment.

The search for the Holy Grail of standardization attracted many disciples. In 1912, Edward L. Thorndike and his graduate student Milo Hillegas created a composition scale (Johnson, 1913) that they claimed could exactly measure and evaluate different means and methods of teaching (Johnson, 1913). Thorndike believed that he could measure student yearly progress with the same precision that he could measure weight, height, or pulse rate.

Thorndike and Hillegas collected and rated 7,000 junior high and high school student writing samples, sorting them into ten levels of writing ability. Their scale consisted of "a series of samples of composition . . . each differing from the preceding by an equal degree of merit" (Thorndike, 1913, p. 534) and was believed to reflect degrees of intelligence. Quite interesting in Thorndike and Hillegas' work is the level of rater variability. Out of 7,000 essays rated, Thorndike and Hillegas used only 21 as samples for the final scale since those were the only essays on which readers agreed. This example points to a fundamental problem—the inability of readers to agree on a definition of good writing. This is significant, for if readers cannot agree or if they agree so infrequently, how then can a test claim to measure ability and, perhaps more important, how can there be a valid standard? Even more discouraging is the fact that these few writing samples "were to serve as standards for all populations *regardless of the background of the writers or the constraints of the topic*" (italics added) (Elliot, Plata, & Zelhart, 1990, p. 29). Despite these major flaws, the orthodoxy of standardization had political appeal and soon gained a position of dominance in education. However, during this time, the focus was still on actual writing. But that was soon to change.

During World War I (between September 1917 and March 1918), the War Department needed to assign 600,000 draftees to appropriate job categories. Robert M. Yerkes, head of the American Psychological Association, developed a multiple choice test to assess the recruits and, in so doing, became the father of large-scale testing in the United States (Elliot, 2005). Subsequent to the development of the multiple choice format, objective tests were introduced for college admissions (Dubois, 1970; Elliot, 2005): "Not surprisingly, instructors liked the 'new examinations' because they were far more comprehensive than earlier methods of testing and because the chance of personal favoritism influencing scores was practically eliminated" (Dubois, 1970, pp. 76–77). In addition, machines scored the tests, making scoring cheap and easy. It is easy to see how budgetary constraints coupled with the call for efficiency in education caused the (temporary) demise of the direct assessment of writing—the veneration of efficiency in cost and time heralded the birth of the "objective" writing test.

The introduction of large-scale writing assessment shifted testing in the United States (another wave) and, along with current-traditional rhetoric, made way for the first experiments in required basic (remedial) writing instruction at the college level (Kasden & Hoeber, 1980).

Developmental programs focused on study habits in the 1930s, on reading in the 1940s, and on the underachiever's total personality in the 1960s—all notions centered on deficit theory. Deficit theory, based on conservative definitions of literacy, focuses on the belief that students come to a curriculum deficient, unable to use a discourse of privilege when communicating, devoid of culture and language, needing to be filled with officially sanctioned knowledge.

Under the influence of deficit theory, writing research focused primarily on the effect specific modes of grammar instruction had on the final written product (Shaughnessy, 1977). Researchers at the time believed that finding a better method of instruction, one based on usage, structure, and correct form, was the most efficient way to improve final product (Hairston, 1982). The outcome of this limited definition is often what is called a *border pedagogy* (Soliday, 2002). Border pedagogies are most often full of tedious and unrelated content (e.g., decontextualized grammar worksheets in a writing class) that labels marginalized students (students on the borders—usually minority language students) deficient. The transfer of this content to students is thus "a celebration of the status quo which downplays nontraditional student culture and the problem of social inequality" (Shor, 1992, p. 32). This is clearly not a great scenario for the second language writer.

Deficit theory led to approaches designed to produce error-free writing. Lessons focused on decontextualized instruction in grammar with no explicit transfer of these skills to the act of composing; unfortunately, teachers expected students to produce not only a grammatically correct product, but somehow a thoughtful, logical one as well (Hairston, 1982). Despite this expectation, teachers regarded content as secondary, if regarded at all, and instructors assessed students' texts primarily at the surface level. They pointed out (but perhaps didn't explain) grammatical problems and errors in usage, often in a sea of red ink. Feedback, if given at all, was full of cryptic comments that students found impossible to translate and use (e.g., the oft-cited "awk"). Consequently, many students became discouraged. Because of noncontextualized and imprecise feedback, most students knew no more than they did when they began an assignment. Not surprisingly, some students developed an increasing dread of subsequent assignments and a strong dislike for writing.

There were still other problems with writing instruction. Prior to the 1960s in the United States, the composition community was not validated. For that matter, it was almost nonexistent. New faculty felt condemned to teach composition while waiting for the next coveted literature appointment (Berlin, 1987; Newkirk, 1994). However, starting in the 1960s and 1970s, a major shift occurred. Faculty again engaged in determining the theory and practice of writing and writing assessment and "rejected product-oriented instruction, adopting process-oriented instruction in its stead" (Crowley, 1996, p. 64). Emig (1971) helped us understand how to better teach (and thereby assess) writing by studying what students do when they write. Emig's groundbreaking research initiated the process-over-product movement. Her work "identified the complex nature of the composing process and raised questions about past approaches to the teaching of writing" (Zamel, 1982, p. 195). Emig's research revealed that writers use writing as an instrument of exploration through which they determine meaning, the process through which they try to make sense of it, and how they learn from the experience (Cooper, 1984). The *Process Approach* was born. Teachers began to use this pedagogy in their classrooms, replacing a focus on correctness with a focus on what people do as they write and how to, through a series of revisions, make meaning through writing.

For a time, process was everything; indeed, teachers became almost evangelistic in their zeal for it. However, they soon began to see faults with their narrowly focused worship at the process altar. In fact, Rose (1981) questioned some process models—he termed them *stage* models as in writing in stages. Rose saw these models as not only inaccurate but also misleading and narrowly conceived. Rose saw the steps as "reductionistic schema" (p. 68) that ignored the recursiveness of the process. However, the process approach showed that writing is a teachable skill (a vitally important point, especially for L2 writers) and is the result of a highly individualized and very complex set of processes. In the years following, the composition field evolved from recognition of these processes, to partial understanding and acceptance of the classroom as a site of democratic action (Shannon, 1995) and inclusion of concerns for the composition classroom as a site of cultural conflict (Shor, 1997).

A History of the Field

Conflict and democratic action figure prominently in writing assessment as well. Consistently, the field of writing assessment has been a site of tension. Although it is sometimes unfair and probably polarizing and simplistic to set up dichotomies of this sort, for the most part, the tensions are primarily between classroom instructors and composition theorists concerned with more organic forms of assessment and psychometricians more concerned with the ability to scientifically and statistically quantify writing. Further, the tenets of a democratic classroom—involving students, regularly and in developmentally appropriate ways, in shared decision-making designed to increase their responsibility and participation in helping to make the classroom a good place to be and learn—are opposite the kinds of writing assessment usually favored by large-scale assessment specialists. However, advances in humanizing writing assessment were on the horizon.

At the very beginning of the process movement, in 1961 in Princeton, NJ, the Educational Testing Service (ETS) published Diederich, French, and Carlton's *Factors in Judgments of Writing Ability* (ETS Research Bulletin 61-15). Using a statistical procedure called *factor analysis,* they condensed 55 categories of comments into five factors: ideas, form, flavor, mechanics, and wording. This was the genesis of what has become the five-point rubric (Broad, 2003) now so ubiquitous.

At about the same time, Godshalk, Swineford, and Coffman were working on the form and scoring of the English Composition Test, an objective test that included one passage to be line-edited. Godshalk proposed that, for the first time, the College Entrance Examination Board (CEEB) and ETS attempt to assess writing through writing (Elliot, 2005). Godshalk and his colleagues, aware of Diederich, French, and Carlton's five factors of writing ability, began experimenting with a new process they called *holistic scoring*. The culmination of the proposal—The Measurement of Writing Ability, 1966—is an important landmark in the development of writing assessment. Because of the psychometric inclination of the researchers, it is not surprising that the study showed the predictive validity and reliability of assessing writing by using objective or indirect measures; however, the big breakthrough, at least in the eyes of many writing teachers, was the claim of slight enhancement of validity and reliability by the addition of a short, holistically scored essay; for the first time in a long time, writing ability was going to be measured by asking people to write.

ETS performed further work on holistic scoring, and in the 1970s, White (1995), a strong advocate of essay testing over decontextualized multiple choice assessments, worked with several English faculty and testing company employees in the development of "holistic scoring methods that allowed quick, economical, and reasonably reliable rankings on large numbers of test papers" (p. 31). It is important to note here that always at the heart of the argument against direct assessment of writing were the quantifiable notions of reliability and validity. It is equally important (and quite fascinating) to note that many years before the SAT included a writing component, the Test of English as a Foreign Language (TOEFL®), a required test for any international student seeking admission to an American university, *did* include writing. This fact seems to indicate that second language writing experts, perhaps because many were language assessment specialists, recognized the value of assessing writing through writing.

In later years, many compositionists began to dismiss "one-shot" essay testing (at least as a means of assessing writing in the classroom) in favor of portfolio assessment, but White (1995) called attention to the important role the essay test played in the history and development of writing assessment; further, because they actually developed a holistic scale to rate actual writing, White credits large-scale testing specialists for improving writing assessment. At last, psychometricians admitted that writing could be assessed through actual writing.

When compositionists turned to the portfolio, they realized that although portfolio assessment might be a more authentic and preferred method of assessment, it too has drawbacks. Chief among them (particularly when used for placement) are the lack of resources: time, energy, and money, factors always in short supply. However, the portfolio and its subsequent withholding of *summative* assessment (an actual grade rather than formative feedback on a series of drafts) is now a central notion in many L1 and L2 writing classrooms And, when properly implemented, portfolios work very well, with advocates (Elbow & Belanoff, 1997; Hamp-Lyons, 2006; Hirvela & Sweetland, 2005) arguing that students might be compelled to engage in real writing for real audiences and real purposes.

The Influence of Science and Measurement on L2 Writing Assessment

Language testing theory assumes that language is a system of communication habits, which can be tested systematically. Spolsky's (1978) history delineates the emergence of that theoretical basis. The history concerns three periods—the pre-scientific, the psychometric-structuralist, and the integrative-sociolinguistic. It is Spolsky's description of the psychometric-structuralist era that is most interesting and clearly outlines the measurement communities' entry into language assessment. In the psychometric-structuralist era, two sets of experts interacted—educational measurement specialists and structural linguists—both believing that testing could be made "precise, objective, reliable, and scientific" (p. vi). Together these two groups produced "a number of well-designed, standardized tests" (p. vii) because each group had a complementary expertise—testing or language—that, when coupled, fostered the creation of something that, in the minds of psychometricians, the first, pre-scientific period, lacked: what they perceived to be highly reliable and valid testing. The psychometric-structuralist believed that knowing a language involved a set of behaviors that could be assessed through discrete structure tests. This proclivity for behaviorism indeed influenced assessment. Huot (1996) remarks that historically writing assessment has been the domain of measurement experts and, for the most part, has been "developed, constructed, and privatized by the measurement community as a technological apparatus whose inner workings are known only to those with specialized knowledge" (p. 549). The same holds true for second language writing assessment. Still today in L2 writing, much assessment is often delegated to language testers, particularly large-scale assessment, evidence that at least a part of our field believes that language skills can only be tested systematically.

Several events facilitated the test development community's dominance in writing assessment. One is that teachers "defaulted" (White, 2001) or did not develop the field in a coherent fashion. Teachers did not create uniform standards or a vocabulary so specialized that it marginalized others. Therefore, because they focused on reliability and validity, the measurement community was the one that defined the field. Unlike teachers, the measurement community possessed extensive financial backing and/or the ability to commercialize their products rapidly, and they recognized the international and financial implications of their work. Finally, the measurement community made coherent and convincing arguments to political and business communities regarding the need for standardization even at the expense of teacher autonomy. Teachers remained reticent in the face of assessment; they felt, and many still feel, marginalization and intimidation—intended or otherwise—from language testing agencies.

Although this period was followed by the integrative-sociolinguistic period beginning in about 1961 with Carroll's (2003) argument for communicative competence and challenges to the "linguistic validity of discrete test items" (p. ix), remnants of the psychometric-structuralist period remain.

Currently, components of these psychometric-structuralist inclinations prevail in some composition classrooms. For instance, even though the process movement influenced L2 writing in much the same way as it did L1 writing (Silva, 1993), what happens when teachers who are unprepared to teach second language writers are confronted with a class of students who have seemingly insurmountable surface-level writing problems? The first urge is to teach decontextualized grammar and return to a product-centered approach to writing instruction and a product-centered, discrete-item means of assessing writing. Unfortunately, this methodology is more prevalent than we would like to admit (Crusan, 2004), but maybe not all that surprising because teachers can be more certain of the answers and do not have to deal with the plethora of nonnative errors. Matsuda (2001) points out the same scientific stance at the roots of second language study to which Spolsky alluded; that is, second language teaching comes out of a tradition that values science. Matsuda cites the work of Fries and Bloomfield who were "interested from early on in developing an approach to language teaching based on the principles of linguistic science" (p. 94) and from the behaviorist leanings of the field in general.

This history offers readers a perspective regarding events that influenced the development of writing assessment, which should help to contextualize these events and the consequential actions. It is interesting to note again the circular nature of history, that movements come in waves, overtaking then-current pedagogical methodologies. Just as the field of second language learning has moved from one method to another, so too has the field of writing assessment.

Currently, many issues surround writing assessment. Of particular concern is large-scale assessment, especially for second language writers. Further concerns focus on placement and the return to objective testing for placement at many institutions. Together with these issues is a new and, as Hamp-Lyons (2001) suggests, fourth wave—computer-assisted scoring of essays, the topic of Chapter 7.

Suggestions for Teachers

1. In the writing program in which you teach/study, what placement methods are used? To find out, make an appointment with the WPA. Before your appointment, make a list of questions. Include questions about the history of the program, what political movements/philosophies might have influenced the method of assessment used for placement in the program, budgetary constraints of the program, the WPA's assessment philosophy. What kinds of conclusions can you draw from the information you have found? Why?
2. The strength of a writing program often lies in its assessment techniques. What kinds of assessment does your writing program engage in? How often does your program engage in re-examining the ways in which it assesses student writing? In my opinion, consistent program re-evaluation is a mark of a good writing program. Further, the involvement of faculty in the examination of program methodology is a major strength. Study your program. Find out what methods of assessment are used and the level of faculty involvement in decisions that affect the teaching and assessing of writing at your institution.

Suggestions for Further Reading

For an exhaustive history of writing assessment in the United States, see Norbert Elliot's 2005 book, *On a Scale: A Social History of Writing Assessment* (New York: Peter Lang).

Chapter 2

An Overview of the Tools of Writing Assessment

Assessment should serve one primary purpose: to improve student learning.
—Bob Peterson, editor, *Rethinking Schools*

Just as carpenters need specialized tools to perform carpentry tasks well, writing teachers also require a focused set of tools to help them assess their students' writing. But first, in order to use those tools well, teachers need to ask themselves questions about assessment and about their students. Some of the most relevant questions are:

- Who are my students?
- What are their specific needs?
- For what purpose(s) am I assessing them?

Knowing the purpose for assessing writing is vital. Additionally, teachers should be cognizant of what I call the rules of writing assessment; I refer to these rules (see page 33) as my creed because I believe that, as a teacher, I need to be accountable to my students for the grades I give them, for the feedback I provide during the stages of writing, and for the information I supply to them about assignments and the assessment of those assignments.

Chapter 2 discusses the purposes for writing assessment and some writing assessment rules, and describes a number of specialized tools including standards, objectives, reliability, validity, washback or impact, rubrics, and writing assignments for different purposes of assessing writing.

Purposes for Assessing Writing

There are many reasons to assess writing. In large part, writing assessment is used to place students into appropriate courses, to give feedback, to give students grades, to determine whether or not they can exit from a program, to verify proficiency, and to evaluate programs. Although program assessment is beyond the scope of this book, it is, nonetheless, an important topic (see O'Neill, Moore, & Huot, 2009, for a comprehensive examination of program evaluation). Since these assessment purposes are high-stakes in nature—they have consequences for our students—it is very important to follow rigorous standards to guarantee that our assessments are valid, fair, and appropriate to the context and purposes for which they are designed.

Purposes for Writing Assessment

Placement: to determine what class a student should take; to separate students into appropriate levels

Diagnosis: to find out what students know, what they need to work on, if they have been properly placed; usually done at the beginning of a class

Aptitude: to determine readiness, innate ability, or skill

Achievement/Progress: to determine what students have learned, what they are able to do as a result of instruction

Proficiency: much like aptitude; however, the skill may not be innate, but has been taught

Program Evaluation: assessment to determine "student learning generally and how that learning is supported by curricula, instruction, and instructional materials." (O'Neill, Moore, & Huot, 2009, p. 109)

Rules of Writing Assessment

Valdez-Pierce (2000, 2003) supports what I like to call *transparent assessment.* That is, Valdez-Pierce feels students need to know the criteria that will be used to assess their writing and what scoring mechanism, if any, will guide the assessment. Drawing principally on the work of Brown (2004), McNamara & Roever (2006), O'Malley & Valdez-Pierce (1996), and Shohamy (2001), I have created a policy of fairness that I use for all my students. In this case, my idea of fairness is not the notion of "social fairness" (McNamara & Roever, 2006, p. 6), which the authors describe as attention to the biases that either favor or penalize minority test takers.

While the issue of social fairness is crucially important, my notion of fairness is aimed more at the classroom context rather than the context of large-scale assessment. In an attempt to make assessment in every class I teach completely and utterly transparent, there are no secrets. I supply students with anchor papers (student writing samples at all levels used as a benchmark/indicator of rubric traits for a particular prompt or assignment), sample papers, examples of projects, study guides, overviews of test formats, lists of criteria and rubrics. And when I provide my students with criteria and rubrics, as advocated by Valdez-Pierce (2000), these instruments are *always* created specifically for the assignment in question. Rarely do I use a specific rubric for more than a single assignment. In a nutshell, my students are educated about how they will be assessed and by what criteria. When I talk about writing assessment in particular, I remind my students that assessment is not "of everything about writing all at once, but rather is targeted to objectives" (NCTE Beliefs about Teaching Writing, http://www.ncte.org/positions/statements/writingbeliefs, 2004). Further, I teach my students (undergraduate and graduate students in TESOL®) to do the same thing for their students, and—I am happy to report—my students report back to me that it works, that their students are satisfied to know how they will be evaluated.

Standards

Opinions and positions differ regarding standards. Standards can have pejorative connotation—McNamara and Roever (2006) maintain that standards "have long been used to enforce social values throughout education systems, and tests are the instruments that implement and operationalized such standards" (p. 7). However, the standards reform movement in the United States is an important issue to consider, especially for ESL (LEP) teachers at the K–12 levels. Not only do teachers need to know what the standards are, but they also need to know how to incorporate these standards into their classrooms. At least in K–12 classrooms in the United States, teachers will need to use the standards as their guides in creating curriculum and assessment. Ohio's proficiency standards for writing are shown as an example.

Ohio English Language Proficiency Standards for LEP Students' Writing	
4.	LEP students will develop the English writing skills required both for academic achievement and for communication in socially and culturally appropriate ways.
4.1	Write using appropriate conventions and grammar
4.2	Write for varied purposes and audiences, with appropriate tone and voice, using various media
4.3	Write using the writing process
4.4	Write using a range of vocabulary, sentence structures, and verb tenses

Ohio English Language Proficiency Standards for Limited English Proficient Students, 2007, p. 4.

As these standards show, they are usually described as measures for accountability (O'Malley & Valdez-Pierce, 1996) or goals that students are expected to achieve. Two kinds of standards—content and performance standards, which are very closely connected—are typically used in schools. *Content standards* give information regarding tasks that students should be able to perform at a particular grade level

(Kuhlman, 1999) and are often confused with *objectives.* While objectives identify the kinds of knowledge and skills desired without any indication of individualized or relative success, *content* standards indicate level of student success (O'Malley & Valdez-Pierce, 1996). Performance standards go into much greater depth than content standards by providing three additional items: suggested tasks, sample student work, and teacher commentary on that work. *Performance* standards provide clear expectations for assessment, instruction, and student work. Ohio calls its performance standards *benchmarks.* An example of benchmarks for Standard 4.3, Write Using the Writing Process, is shown.

Ohio Standard 4.3 Benchmarks

BENCHMARKS	GRADE LEVELS			
Intermediate level	K–2	3–5	6–8	9–12
Uses pre-writing strategies to generate and organize ideas for writing about a given topic with extensive support	✓	✓	✓	✓
Edit written work for mechanics and structure to improve fluency, with support	1–2	✓	✓	✓
Judge the quality of writing, with support	1–2	✓	✓	✓
Publish for display and/or sharing using available technology, with support	1–2	✓	✓	✓
Organize and draft a paragraph based on pre-writing activities, with support	2	✓	✓	✓
Review and revise draft paragraphs for content, organization, and vocabulary, with support	2	✓	✓	✓

Ohio English Language Proficiency Standards for Limited English Proficient Students, 2007, p. 73.

New York provides learning standards in the four skills. For example, Standard 4 reads: "Students will listen, speak, read, and write in English for classroom and social interaction." New York then sets performance indicators by grade level. The next example—just one of the twelve performance indicators for Standard 4—demonstrates what students will be able to do and how skills might be assessed:

New York State ESL Learning Standards
STANDARD 4: Performance Indicator 1 for Grades 9–12
Use a variety of oral, print, and electronic forms for social communication and for writing to or for self, applying the conventions of social writing. Such forms include friendly notes, invitations, and electronic messages, diary entries, and notes to self.

English as a Second Language, New York State ESL Learning Standards, Performance Indicators by Grade Level, 2009, p. 119.

ESL content and performance assessment standards have also been developed nationally by TESOL, have been adapted for use in a variety of states, and are regularly updated and evaluated. Additionally, World-Class Instructional Design and Assessment (WIDA), a consortium of states (22 in 2010), collectively designs and implements standards for ELLs. An example of WIDA's Model Performance Indicators is provided.

A Strand of Model Performance Indicators with an Example Topic				
LEVEL 1 ENTERING	LEVEL 2 BEGINNING	LEVEL 3 DEVELOPING	LEVEL 4 EXPANDING	LEVEL 5 BRIDGING
Produce personal word/phrase lists from labeled pictures and check with a partner for edits and revision	Create phrases/short sentences from models and check with a partner for edits and revision	Edit and revise guided writing (e.g., for conventions and structures) based on teacher feedback	Edit and revise writing (e.g., using word processing or rubrics) based on class or peer reviews	Self-assess to edit and revise writing to produce final drafts
Standards Reference Framework: Formative Standard: 2—The language of Language Arts Grade-level cluster: 3–5			Language Domain: Writing Example topic: Editing and revising	

Gottlieb, Cranley, and Cammilleri. *Understanding the WIDA English proficiency standards: A resource guide* (2007, p. RG-15).

Standards are useful tools to help teachers determine what to teach and the order of teaching content; standards also serve as a yardstick to measure student knowledge. For example, in its standards document, Ohio calls the English Language Proficiency Standards "a resource for teachers" (p. v) that "define progressive levels of competence and serve as a guide for teachers in moving limited English proficient students toward proficiency" (p. v). Schools can take standards and use them to design programs that help English language learners (ELLs) develop language proficiency needed for academic achievement and participation in society. The Ohio standards for writing include items such as developing writing skills that are socially and culturally appropriate. Students should be able to work through the writing process, use appropriate conventions and grammar, know how to write for a variety of purposes and audiences, use suitable register, be able to use various media, and be able to manipulate vocabulary, sentence structures, and verb tenses. When viewed this way, standards seem benign and befitting the classroom.

Of course, an overreliance on standards might create lock-step curricula with little room for invention and creativity, definitely a negative outcome. But having guidelines can be positive, if teachers are allowed to interpret those guidelines individually, creating assignments that adhere to the standards but also value and allow the expression of teacher creativity and innovation. As usual though, accountability reigns and the U.S. government has called for the development of more rigorous real-world standards (Kohn, 2000; McNeil, 2000; Monroe, 2006) to be measured by still more standardized tests, thus pushing schools to obtain improved data tools to gauge student achievement, some of which are helpful in finding who needs more help. Teachers need to be ever mindful of who controls what is taught and, in the end, who knows what is best for the students, individually and as a class.

Objectives

Standards are models or bases of comparison, but objectives are purposes, goals, or targets. Often, teachers will state their objectives in their course documents (e.g., syllabi, assignments) and lesson plans. Some examples of course objectives are provided.

For an Introduction to a Linguistics course
This course is designed to give you a basic understanding of certain aspects of the English language, to lead you to investigate your own linguistic tenets and attitudes, and to guide you to the recognition that language is enormously and wondrously complex. Through the acquisition of a theoretical framework, you will be better able to analyze the universal components inherent in language and apply this knowledge to the biological and social contexts of language.

For a TESOL Assessment Course
Assessment is a complicated matter, the scientific and sometimes political scope of which can often put teachers off. With that thought in mind, *TESOL Assessment* will attempt to investigate notions surrounding assessment through teachers' eyes in language that is *utilitarian*, *practical*, and *accessible*. Additionally, we will investigate the many forms of assessment.
The main goals of the course are to enable prospective and practicing ESL/EFL teachers: • to better understand the purposes of assessment • to grasp key concepts and their underlying theories in the field of language assessment • to create authentic assessment tasks in the classroom • to understand that assessment is an integral part of teaching and learning but that it should be ancillary to both • to critically examine issues surrounding assessment and the consequences of assessment.

Additionally, teachers often list daily objectives on the board at the beginning of class to guide students. Objectives are what I like to call SWBATs (**S**tudents **W**ill **B**e **A**ble **T**o); certainly, I did not coin this term, but it has been in my repertoire since my undergraduate days. SWBATs are a wonderful tool for teaching and assessment because what is taught is what is assessed. Plainly, this illustrates that teaching and assessment are intertwined. Everything we do in our classes is a form of assessment, whether formal or informal. SWBATs can guide our day-to-day classrooms, moving us closer to our goals.

Some examples of SWBATs for a writing class are:

At the end of today's class/this week/the term, **S**tudents **W**ill **B**e **A**ble **T**o:
• write a first draft • reread their text for meaning • create coherence with keys terms, pronouns, and synonyms • revise to clarify and refine meaning • effectively assess a peer's text during peer review

Many of these SWBATs can be easily assessed at the end of the class, week, or term, and some can be very informally assessed. For instance, a quick walk around the classroom can be enough to be able to judge students' ability to have produced a first draft of a writing assignment. Another example: the answers to a peer review sheet can be graded to assess students' ability to provide effective evaluation of their peers' work.

Reliability

Another aspect of writing assessment is reliability. There are many different kinds of reliability, including student-related reliability, inter-rater reliability, and test reliability. *Student-related reliability,* for example, is compromised when a student is sick or tired or suffers from any number of physical or psychological problems. *Inter-rater reliability* refers to degree to which the scores of raters agree. *Test reliability* refers to issues with the test itself—length, quality of directions, and content.

In general, *reliability* refers to the degree to which a test is consistent and stable in measuring what it is intended to measure. Most simply put, a test is reliable if it is consistent within itself and across time. To understand the basics of test reliability, imagine a bathroom scale that gives you drastically different readings every time you step on it regardless of whether your have gained or lost weight. This scale would be considered unreliable. So how is reliability a tool for writing assessment? Some might think that reliability has only to do with standardized tests, but no teacher would want to give a test that does not accurately assess a student's knowledge. Such a test would be useless.

Further, reliability is a critically important issue in the rating of essays for any purpose but especially for those purposes that are considered high-stakes, such as placement, passing out of a class, and passing out of a program. If raters are discrepant, the decisions made on behalf of the writer cannot be trusted. Basically, any discussion of reliability is addressing the dependability of a test. Can we depend on a test to give us the same results time after time? To put it in plainer terms, have you ever given a test only to find that students' answers vary wildly? While the problem could rest with the students or with the teacher, quite possibly, the test is not reliable/dependable. That is, it does not deliver the same results time after time. Teachers should be concerned about reliability because, without it, determining what students know is difficult at best.

Scenarios That Produce Unreliable Test Results
You administer a timed essay test in your class as a means of determining students' ability to develop a specific topic through writing. However, the students' essays address topics other than that called for in the prompt—they differ in ways that tell you that no one understood the test question; therefore, the results of your test are unreliable for its purpose.
A teacher asks her students to complete a test of 250 short answer questions within a 55-minute class block. Not one student is able to finish the test. The results of the test are not a true measure of what the students know.
A teacher includes phonetic symbols on his test although he has never introduced them in class. Obviously, students will not perform well on material never presented.
A student comes to school on the day of the standardized test with a temperature of 102. Throughout the test administration, she sits with her head on her desk, unable to answer even the simplest questions.

Validity

As with reliability, there are many different kinds of validity. Some of the major types are content validity, criterion validity, construct validity, face validity, and consequential validity.

Content validity means that the test measures what it is supposed to measure. For instance, if the NFL wants to find out how fast a wide receiver can run, he is asked to run, not to lift a certain amount of weight. And if teachers want to measure how well students can write, certainly they should ask the students to write.

Criterion validity refers to "comparing scores on the test to some criterion other than another test" (Stoynoff & Chapelle, 2005, p. 216). It involves how well a test correlates with another measure—a more concrete criterion. For example, a driving test has some correlation to a person's driving ability. Likewise, a paper and pencil test on public speaking might be validated by actual performance—that is, students giving speeches.

Construct validity relates to theoretical claims that factors such as development, organization, and issues of grammar and mechanics are major components of proficiency in writing. Therefore, a multiple choice instrument testing vocabulary knowledge would lack construct validity as a writing test.

Face validity has to do with the look of the test; that is, does the test look like it can measure what it is supposed to measure? Certainly students would expect a writing test to look a certain way; if the test's appearance does not meet the learners' expectations, the test lacks face validity.

The final, and in my estimation most important, type of validity is *consequential validity.* When we administer a test, we need to be cognizant of the consequences of that test. Such validity is problematic in the socioeconomic context of test-prep due to the inherent bias favoring those students who can afford to pay for the various course and manuals that promise higher scores and (consequently) admission to better schools, access to scholarships, and other educational successes that are usually thought to be based on merit rather than money.

How do we know that a test is showing what we want it to show? Test validity refers to the degree to which the test actually measures what it claims to measure. Test validity is also the extent to which inferences, conclusions, and decisions made on the basis of test scores are appropriate and meaningful. A strong relationship exists between reliability and validity. Test validity is essential to test reliability. If a test is not valid, then its reliability is irrelevant. In other words, if a test is not valid there is no point in discussing reliability because test validity is required before reliability can be considered in any meaningful way. Likewise, if a test is not reliable, it is also not valid.

Practicality

In order for any writing assessment to be effective, it must be practical. Practicality refers to pragmatic issues such as time, money, and ease. If a test is prohibitively expensive, it simply is not practical, no matter how good the test is. If a test takes a student an inordinately long time to complete, it is impractical. The same can be said for a test that is difficult to administer because it is either overly complicated or requires incredibly complex staffing or technology to administer. Once again, in most cases, in most classrooms, and for most institutions, such a test would be extremely impractical.

Washback

In language testing terms, washback is the effect of an assessment on teaching and learning. Messick (1996) defines washback as "the extent to which the introduction and use of a test influences language teachers and learners to do things they would not otherwise do that promote or inhibit language learning" (p. 241). Washback can be either positive or negative. *Positive washback* happens when the results of a test trigger improvement of a course or a syllabus.

Instances of Positive Washback
The introduction of a speaking component on the Test of English as a Foreign Language (TOEFL®) has resulted in the addition of the teaching of speaking in some English as a Foreign Language contexts.
The introduction of a writing component on standardized tests such as the SAT® has, although it may be of the formulaic nature, resulted in more of a focus on actual writing in U.S. high schools.

However, test results may influence curriculum negatively. Witness the aftermath of No Child Left Behind; test results have caused the narrowing of the curriculum in the U.S. K–12 schools, an example of negative washback. Luckily, effects of negative washback do not have to be lasting if they are quickly recognized and remediated.

Instances of Negative Washback
The initiation of the No Child Left Behind Act in U.S. K–12 schools has resulted in the exclusion of courses from the curriculum that are not on the test. (Kohn, 2000)
Aware of the power of tests, policy-makers may use them "to manipulate the educational system and to control curricula and new teaching methods" (Shohamy, Donitsa-Schmidt, and Ferman, 1996, p. 316)
In rare cases, children may develop illnesses, both physcal and psychological, because of extreme pressure to perform well on tests. (Kohn, 2000)

Rubrics

Rubrics can do for a curriculum what objectives do—they can help explain terms and clarify expectations. There are many proponents of rubrics, and there are just as many opponents. For example, Kohn (2006) argues that (perhaps institutionally imposed) rubrics lead to a "standardization" of how teachers "think about student assignments" (pp. 12–13). He admits that rubrics can play a constructive role in assessment, but, he stresses that they must be used in conjunction with other sources and not allowed to drive instruction, which often happens. Broad (2003) and Wilson (2006) caution us about the lure of rubrics and their tendency to narrow assessment. Wilson (2006) considers rubrics potentially damaging and standardizing, confessing that she will not use rubrics because they cannot "capture the nuances of students' writing" (p. 63). Clearly, as in the case of high-stakes testing, writing can be reduced to a formula that shapes instruction and perception of writing. But shunning the rubrics used by high-stakes raters will not help. Rather some rubrics are relevant to help students prepare to move past gatekeepers. They can be "starting points from which we make our own rubrics" (Calkins cited in Spandel, 2006, p. 19).

Rubrics can be powerful tools when they are *created specifically for each assignment;* they are even more powerful when created with students. When this occurs, areas of confusion can be recognized, wording clarified or simplified, and meanings illuminated. Teachers can bring a straw rubric to class and ask students to provide input about what they think is fair, or teachers and students can brainstorm together to create categories and criteria for assignments and rubrics. In these ways, students are more likely to be invested in the assignment and engaged in learning and assessment.

One of the most powerful reasons for using rubrics is that students are less likely to question their grade if the rubric is carefully constructed and if students have been involved in its creation. The use of a well-constructed rubric will justify students' grades for them by clearly showing them ways in which their work will be evaluated and what is expected of them. Further, rubrics allow for more objective and consistent evaluation and provide feedback to teachers regarding instructional effectiveness. Because assessment should never be shrouded in mystery and should always be very explicit, when creating an assignment for students, teachers should take great care to create a rubric that exactly matches the criteria for the assignment.

The three most common rubrics are the *holistic* rubric, the *analytic* rubric, and the *primary trait* rubric. The *holistic* rubric is generally a five- or six-point scale that involves ranking a sample of a student's writing by matching it with another piece in a benchmark series, scoring it for the prominence of certain features (coherence, development) important to that kind of writing, and assigning it a grade. Holistic rating is an impressionistic rating of essays for overall quality and is often used for placing students in composition classes and for assessing writing in large-scale assessments such as the TOEFL® and the SAT®. Interestingly, even-numbered rubrics are preferred because they force the evaluator to place the work at a level above or below the middle.

Example of a Holistic Rubric

4—EXCEEDS CRITERIA	3—MEETS CRITERIA	2—PROGRESSING TO CRITERIA	1—BELOW EXPECTATIONS
Writer provides ample details and examples to support main points	Writer provides adequate details and examples to support main points	Writer includes some details but it is not clear how they are related	Writer includes few details; details unrelated to the text
Writer is able to clearly organize position logically	Writer shows occasional lapses in organization and logic	Writer shows many lapses in organization and logic	Writer shows inability to logically organize writing
Writer uses language effectively and correctly with engaging language choice for the audience and writing purpose	Writer uses language effectively with occasional lapses in word choice for audience and purpose	Writer uses language ineffectively with word choice inappropriate for audience and purpose	Writer has limited or inappropriate vocabulary and word choice
Writer follows the conventions of English with very few errors	Writer generally follows the conventions of English with occasional errors	Writer generally does not follow the conventions of Standard English	Writer is unable to follow the conventions of Standard English

Adapted from www.abet.org/assessment.shtml

While the holistic rubric provides "fast evaluation, relatively high inter-rater reliability, and applicability to writing across many different disciplines" (Brown, 2004, p. 242), its disadvantages must be weighed when deciding to use the holistic scale. For example, the scale may not apply to all genres of writing. Holistic rubrics (especially those of the standardized test variety) seem to prize the four- or five-paragraph essay, which is predominantly descriptive or expository; further, holistic scales reduce writing to a single score. The disadvantages of a single score especially play out in the classroom and in the school district. One singular score is simply that—a single score that can provide information about how a student performed during one instance in time. Extrapolating that single score to a global assessment of student performance and ability is naïve and often unjust.

An *analytic* rubric includes a more detailed analysis, usually based on a scale or checklist of prominent features or characteristics of a piece of writing. The features selected for evaluation vary according to the context of the specific writing assignment, the audience, and the purpose for writing. One of the most well-known analytic rubrics is the ESL Composition Profile (Jacobs, Hartfiel, Hughey, & Wormuth, 1981). Another equally excellent analytic rubric, a more up-to-date adaptation of the ESL Composition Profile, is available in Ferris & Hedgcock (2005). While the analytic rubric offers more positive washback—"the effect of testing on teaching and learning" (Hughes, 2003, p. 1), arithmetical scores are still inadequate for helping students become better writers (Brown, 2004).

An assignment for a reflection letter and the accompanying analytic rubric are provided on page 47. Notice that the assignment includes the criteria on which writers will be evaluated (see page 48).

The final type of rubric, the primary trait rubric—and a variant, the multiple-trait rubric (Hamp-Lyons, 1991)—analyzes certain language use and scores for one trait (e.g. organization, or the correct use of the past tense). These rubrics are useful for assessing L2 learners' proficiency and growth in writing; they are potentially more informative than the other types of rubrics because they are more focused and are particularly helpful in the classroom for diagnosing student writing abilities. Although primary trait scoring looks at only one trait in writing, other features might be covertly or even unconsciously rated using this method. However, primary trait scoring allows writer and assessor to focus on function (see page 49).

Assignment

<table>
<tr><td>English 112
Reflection Letter 2</td></tr>
<tr><td>In this reflection letter talk about what you have done and what you have learned about academic reading and writing this quarter and about yourself as an academic English reader and writer. Use specific details from your experience in this classroom (activities we did, discussions, lecture topics, examples from your writing, etc.) to support your answers to the following questions:</td></tr>
<tr><td>• STRENGTHS/WEAKNESSES: What are your strengths as an English reader/writer? What are some of your weaknesses as a reader/writer? (Refer back to your first reflection letter and comment on whether these things have changed or not.)</td></tr>
<tr><td>• LEARNING: What specifically have you learned that is new? What have you learned again that you already knew but either didn't understand or weren't using? How did you learn these things?</td></tr>
<tr><td>• ACTIVITIES: Consider the activities we have done this quarter: summary and response papers, reading articles, compare/contrast essay, grammar logs, in-class timed writing practice, reflection letters.
◦ What has been most challenging for you so far? Why?
◦ What has been the least challenging for you so far? Why?
◦ What has been the most helpful for you? Why? What strategies or tools have been helpful for you?
◦ What has been the least helpful for you? Why? What strategies or tools have not been helpful for you?</td></tr>
<tr><td>• PERFORMANCE: Rate your participation/ performance (honestly — your rating does not affect your grade, but your honesty does). Have you given your full effort? What have you done well? What could you have done better?</td></tr>
<tr><td>• RESPONSE: How have you dealt with the challenges of this class? How do you plan to deal with future challenges? Do you plan to do things the same as you have been doing, or is there something different you plan to do? What aspects of your reading/writing have you improved? What would you still like to improve? How do you plan to do that?</td></tr>
<tr><td>Requirements:
• The letter should be at least 2 full pages and formatted like all our class papers.</td></tr>
<tr><td>Expectations [Criteria on Rubric]:
• Identify your strengths/weaknesses as an English reader/writer.
• Explain what you have learned in this class.
• Describe how class elements have affected your learning.
• Evaluate your progress/work to this point.
• Identify areas for improvement and set goals for the remainder of the quarter.
• Give specific answers & provide examples.
• Fully develop explanations.
• Meet criteria for well-organized & proofread essay.</td></tr>
</table>

Rubic

Reflection Letter 2	0	1	2	3	4	Points
Addresses (some of) the questions on the assignment handout						
Describes writer's progress as a writer/reader						
Evaluates progress/work to this point						
Discusses strengths and weaknesses						
Asks questions about reading/writing						
Formatted per class guidelines						
Fully develops explanations (length & content — 1.5–2 pp)						
Meets criteria for a well-organized & proofread essay						
					Total	
					Grade	

From Charis Nims, Wright State University ESL Composition instructor, for this assignment.

Primary Trait Rubric: Vocabulary

Criteria	Level	Score
Excellent to Very Good The document shows sophisticated range with effective word and/or idiom form, choice, and usage. It shows word form mastery and an appropriate register.	**20–18**	
Good to Average The document shows adequate range, with occasional errors of word and/or idiom form, choice, and usage but meaning not obscured.	**17–14**	
Fair to Poor The document shows limited range with frequent errors of word and/or idiom form, choice, and usage. Its meaning is confused or obscured.	**13–10**	
Very poor The document is essentially a translation. It shows little knowledge of English vocabulary, idioms, and word form.	**9–1**	
Comments		
Total Score		

Inter American University of Puerto Rico,
Ponce Campus, 2002.

While it is important to use a rubric of some sort when assessing the writing of our second language students, Haswell and Wysche-Smith (1994) remind us that "a rating system should use the expertise of teachers rather than just obedience to a holistic rubric" (p. 222). However, all teachers would be wise to be aware of their own personal "rubric in the head," a set of criteria or standards that, even though they have not been overtly shared with students, often underlie all the criteria upon which students will be graded. A good rubric, therefore, is as important for the teacher as it is for the student because it forces teachers to focus on the explicit evaluation criteria.

Writing Assignments

Writing assignments are a critical part of any writing class. Basically, a good assignment should include an assignment sheet; a schedule with due dates for drafts, conferences, and peer review; accompanying materials and/or readings; and an explicit description of the ways in which the assignment will be evaluated. Often students complain that they do not know what their teacher wants. To prevent these complaints, include information such as expected paper length, citation requirements, formatting requirements, penalties for late work, and acceptable topics. A few of my own assignments and accompanying rubrics are shown on pages 51–54. While they are not specifically for writing classes, they are examples of assignments that set specific criteria that are then reflected in the scoring rubrics.

My fundamental message is that the form of assessment must be determined for each specific assignment; one type of assessment does not fit all circumstances. Students become invested in the multidimensional aspects of writing when the criteria for assessment are clear and when students are involved in the creation of rubrics and other assessment tools.

For a Textbook Review in a Practices & Materials Class:

TEXTBOOK REVIEW ASSIGNMENT Due July 9, 20xx
Please choose a current ESL/EFL textbook. Then, reflect on the issues below that a teacher should contemplate when considering a text. Write a brief (no more than 500 words) book review that provides a description and evaluation of the book and discusses the items below.
1. **AUDIENCE:** For whom is the book intended *according to the author*? Does it appear to be appropriate for this audience?
2. **AIMS:** What are the goals of the textbook *according to the author*? Does it appear that the text meets these goals?
3. **CONTENT:** What language points/skills are taught? What types of texts (conversations, lectures, magazine articles) are used? What subject matter, if any, is used (science, culture, etc.)? How is the material organized (structures, functions, topics, etc.)? What, if any, cultural assumptions are implicit in the text?
4. **METHODOLOGY:** What theory of second language acquisition learning appears to underlie the text? What exercise types are included (multiple choice questions, fill-in-the-blanks, writing, discussion)?
5. **OTHER:** Do you like the layout? Are other materials required or provided? Are there indices, appendices, and/or glossaries?
6. **EVALUATION:** What is the major strength of the text? What is its major weakness, in your opinion? What would you suggest to improve the text, or how might you advise a teacher who is considering using the text?
Other important information: • 500 word limit • No late work accepted • Use APA citation style • Must be word processed • Use standard one-inch margins and double spacing

Accompanying Rubric — Given to Students with the Textbook Review Assignment

English 474/674: TEFL Practices & Materials Book Review Evaluation Form						
This book review considers the following:						
Includes complete bibliographic information in APA format: author, year of pub, title, pub place, publisher, # of pages	0	1	2	3	4	5
Includes level/audience for which text is appropriate	0	1	2	3	4	5
Discusses the goals of the text and their appropriateness	0	2	4	6	8	10
Describes content/topics used	0	1	2	3	4	5
Discusses sequencing of activities	0	1	2	3	4	5
Discusses cultural assumptions of the text	0	1	2	3	4	5
Discusses methodology underlying the text	0	2	4	6	8	10
Details kinds of activities	0	1	2	3	4	5
Discusses the layout of the text	0	1	2	3	4	5
Discusses index, answer key, appendix	0	1	2	3	4	5
Outlines major strengths of the text	0	2	4	6	8	10
Delineates major weaknesses of the text	0	2	4	6	8	10
Discusses improvements that might be made in the text	0	2	4	6	8	10
Includes advice to teachers considering adoption of text	0	2	4	6	8	10
Discusses work's relative significance in context of current theory and practice	0	2	4	6	8	10
Book review is appropriate length	0	1	2	3	4	5
Book review is both descriptive and evaluative	0	1	2	3	4	5
COMMENTS						
TOTAL SCORE						/120
KEY: 0 = missing; 1 = poor/scant; 2 = fair; 3 = average; 4 = above average; 5 = extremely well-done						

Note that several categories are weighted heavier than others.

Final Project Assignment in a TESOL Assessment Class

<table>
<tr><td>English 487/687 — TESOL Assessment
Final Project</td></tr>
<tr><td>Using what you have learned in the course, design an authentic assessment and write a rationale for that assessment. Include context, student population, goals, scoring criteria, and an original scoring procedure if applicable. You will need to find a real context in which you can <u>pilot</u> your assessment. You will be reporting on the success or failure of your assessment and any scoring rubric that you have designed to score the assessment. See below for specific criteria.</td></tr>
<tr><td>Context: A context is the circumstances or events that form the environment within which something exists or takes place. So . . . for what context will you be designing your assessment? The context must be <u>real</u>. Please contact any of the following people who teach ESL classes here at Wright State:
[LIST OF INSTRUCTORS]
When you contact a person, explain what you would like to do — design an assessment specifically for their students — assuring them that it's OK for them NOT to participate. You should find out what the students in their classes are doing, what the teacher might like help with, if you can observe the class for a session or two to see who the students are and what needs they have. You should develop an assessment that is formative, authentic, helpful to the students and the teacher, and has positive washback.</td></tr>
<tr><td>In a short report (both written and oral) of your assessment design project, you will discuss (in any order):</td></tr>
<tr><td>1. Context: In what context was your assessment administered? Describe the course, the teacher, the goals of the course.</td></tr>
<tr><td>2. Purpose of the assessment: What is/are the purpose(s) for which the assessment is being developed? What are you assessing?</td></tr>
<tr><td>3. Student population: Who took the assessment? What skills or abilities were measured?</td></tr>
<tr><td>4. Rationale for the assessment: Why are you assessing this population in the manner in which you are assessing them? Provide a rationale, based on research, regarding the tasks performed.</td></tr>
<tr><td>5. Theoretical perspective of the assessment: How does the assessment reflect assessment theory in regard to the selection, arrangement, and methods of assessing content? You should include procedures for ensuring authenticity, representativeness (the extent to which the assessment accurately samples the behavioral domain of interest), and comprehensiveness of the assessment content.</td></tr>
<tr><td>6. Directions: Specify the instructions that were given to those taking the assessment. Directions must be clear and easy to understand. (Use sample items where necessary to ensure appropriate response to the questions.)</td></tr>
<tr><td>7. The assessment: Include the actual assessment. Present it in your paper (in an appendix) in the form in which it appeared when you administered it to examinees.</td></tr>
<tr><td>8. Scoring: Indicate how the assessment was scored. Provide a key or scoring rubric. If relevant, provide instructions for training of raters. Include a rationale and description of any weighting scheme for components of the assessment. For example, if you are developing an assessment of oral proficiency and wish to weight pronunciation heavier than fluency or comprehensibility, please explain your rationale for doing so.</td></tr>
<tr><td>9. What did you learn?: Briefly discuss the success or failure of your assessment, the purpose, the rubric. Report on the actual administration of the assessment. What did you learn from completing the project? What might you do differently if you were starting over? How might this knowledge help you in the future?</td></tr>
<tr><td>10. Reference Section: Please use APA style.</td></tr>
<tr><td>IN OTHER WORDS: WHY DO IT? — HOW TO DO IT? — HOW TO SCORE IT? — WHAT TOOLS TO USE? — WHAT WENT RIGHT? — WHAT WENT WRONG? — WHY?</td></tr>
</table>

Assessment Project Rubric

English 487/687: TESOL Assessment ***Final Project***						
NAME						
REQUIRED CONTENTS	0	1	2	3	4	5
Description of context						
Purpose of the test (x2)						
Student population						
Rationale for the test (x2)						
Reflective of theory (x2)						
Authentic procedures						
Clarity of test directions						
Actual test included						
Scoring rubric included						
Discussion of success/failure of the test (x2)						
Discussion of success/failure of the rubric (x2)						
What was learned						
Citation of sources						
Discussion of test creation						
Clear adaptation of materials						
ADDITIONAL COMMENTS						
COLUMN SCORES						
TOTAL SCORE						/100
KEY: : 0 = missing; 1 = poor; 2 = adequate; 3 = good; 4 = outstanding; 5 = stellar; x2 = double weight						

Suggestions for Teachers

1. Conduct an informal survey at your school that examines the use of assessment criteria and rubrics among the faculty. Your findings might help support the need for writing assessment workshops at your institutions.
2. Choose a teacher or professor from another field/ discipline. Interview him or her about attitudes, beliefs, and philosophy of the teaching of writing. Ask him or her what constitutes good writing and how he or she views assessment. How do these beliefs acknowledge or dispute current writing and writing assessment theory?

Chapter 3
Designing Assignments and Rubrics

All assessment is a perpetual work in progress.
—Linda Suske

When I talk with ESL and EFL teachers, I am surprised—whether they teach kindergarten or college—to learn that although they constantly evaluate their students, both formally and informally, few think of themselves as assessment experts. Yet, imagine the desk of any elementary teacher without rolls of colorful stickers proclaiming "Nice job!" or "This is much better!" Or consider any university composition teacher at the end of the term, barricaded in her office by stacks of ungraded student portfolios. Certainly, assessment is part of a teacher's job. Unfortunately, assessment remains the job all teachers love to hate; in fact, of all of a teacher's many duties, the task of evaluating students' writing is perhaps one of the most distressing and time-consuming. However, when teachers are armed with assessment techniques, are skilled rubric creators, and can articulate their criteria to their students, assessing writing becomes a fair enterprise and a much less formidable task.

When I discuss writing assessment in this chapter, I am also referring to all the different kinds of teacher-made writing assignments, whether they are completed in class or as an assignment done outside of class. I am also referring to assessment that is both *formative* (in that it is linked to instruction—students use this feedback to improve their writing) and *summative* (where a final grade is given to quantify relative or absolute student achievement). The forms of assessment range from feedback on early drafts, to responding to journals or response/reaction papers, to grading final products—let's call these instances **little *a*** (assessment) as opposed to BIG A, or the large-scale writing assessments that often come in the form of standardized tests, which will be discussed in Chapter 5. Formative assessment affords teachers multiple opportunities to read student work, thereby supporting students in all stages of the writing process.

Personal Experience as a Student

Clearly, the past years have seen an improvement in the way teachers assess writing. But for me, memories of my own early experiences with writing remain vivid and painful. In 1967, as a freshman in college enrolled in a first-year English course, I was repeatedly instructed to 'write an essay about' the piece of literature we had recently read and discussed in class. The assignment was usually a single statement such as "discuss the use of metaphor in *The Great Gatsby*." The professor offered no additional criteria. I floundered every week, writing as best I could with the limited understanding of an 18-year-old who had never critically analyzed literature (or little else, for that matter). On Fridays, I dutifully turned in my papers; on Mondays, the professor handed them back. Invariably, across the top of my paper in red were brief comments such as "mediocre analysis," or "needs work," followed by C+ or B–. I received no other feedback. Once I remember visiting the professor's office to ask for help to make my analysis better. My instructor sternly warned that I needed to dig deeper and think harder about what I was reading, assuming that I understood what this meant. I was not instructed or guided about how I was supposed to accomplish such a formidable task. While I failed to gain a love of writing from this particular professor (or any other professor at this particular institution), I did gain a perspective on teaching that has remained with me, one that does not assume knowledge but, instead, prizes a clear and explicit connection between teaching and assessment.

Personal Experience as a Teacher

It probably isn't surprising to learn that I dropped out of college at age 19. Seventeen years later, I returned to another institution to finish my bachelor of science degree in education. When I first became an educator, I knew little about teaching. I can't remember any of my undergraduate professors talking to me about teaching in the ways that I talk to my students about it. So I made a lot of mistakes (no doubt to the detriment of my students), but I learned from them. In my first developmental English class, blasé to a fault and perhaps more than a little naïve, I asked my students to write a paragraph about "anything they wanted to write about"—my first (and very costly) mistake. I gave them no other instructions. That was the entire assignment. I also gave them no information about how I would assign a grade to that paragraph.

I collected the paragraphs during the next class and excitedly took them home to read. I was a teacher. I had given my students an assignment, and they did it! I guess I thought that was all it took to be a teacher, and I felt powerful and accomplished. Those feelings quickly dissipated as soon as I began reading the paragraphs my students had written. My heart sank as I realized I could not hold my students accountable for *anything.* Somehow I realized that without having assigned any criteria, my hands were tied. I had not told my students what I would be looking for; I had not been accountable to my students, so I could not hold them accountable for any of the numerous issues in their writing. I quickly learned that I needed to tell my students what they were supposed to do. I needed to be far more explicit when making assignments. Of course, my assessment techniques evolved over time. It took much reading, many workshops and conferences, and lots of trial and error as I progressively developed a more honed sense of the process of creating nuanced, fair, and transparent assignments and assessments. Still, my assessment of writing (or of anything I teach) is a work in progress, one that I attempt to improve over time.

I have discovered many things in my years of teaching at the K–8, high school, community college, and university levels. One of my most important discoveries is the notion of *cultural capital* (Bourdieu, 1996, 2005; Delpit, 2006). Many university professors, especially, assume all students have similar backgrounds. However, if I learned one thing in my undergraduate teaching courses, it was that I should never assume a student's base of knowledge. Further, if students do not have the knowledge, you must provide it. This notion of cultural capital (Delpit, 1988, 2006) is especially applicable to second language writers, a diverse population.

Delpit (1988, 2006) writes about the education of African-American children. She notes that for many of these children, school is a world in which they cannot operate because they lack the understanding of how school works. They can't *do* school (Johnson, 1999). For example, in a writing class, students may be surprised when the teacher returns an assignment in which they are penalized for incorrect punctuation. When they inquire, the answer is often, "This is an English class (or this is college), so of course punctuation counts." Students may remark that they weren't told *what* counts. If you want to "count" something when assessing a writing assignment, then you need to tell your students what counts. This is especially important in L2 writing courses, as many teachers are encountering large refugee populations that include students who often have little idea about negotiating school in general, let alone the specific goals and nuances of writing assessment. These students need to be brought gently into the system. As educators, we need to remember the affective as well as the cognitive; Krashen's (1987) notion of lowering the affective filter in order to engage students is still valid.

Considerations in Designing Assessments

When designing assessments for the writing classroom, teachers should first consider the specific reasons they are using writing in their classrooms. Remember the pedagogical role of assessment in the teaching of composition: responding to and evaluating student writing are crucial to successful ESL writing instruction (Ferris & Hedgcock, 2005).

For the purposes of this book, I will be considering classes geared toward *instruction* in second language academic writing: writing essays in genres expected in the classroom; research paper skills, including citation style; and the appropriate use and integration of the work of others. Certainly other purposes for writing, such as note-taking, emailing, journal entries, essay exams, peer evaluation, and letter writing, are important, but these are beyond the scope of this chapter.

Although the standards movement in the United States has brought concern for teacher autonomy, it has also provided teachers with useful guidelines around which to structure curriculum. The TESOL standards provide a good example (www.tesol.org/s_tesol). In its *ESL Standards for Pre-K–12 Students: Grades 9–12,* TESOL first states the goal and standard—what students should be able to do generally:

Goal 2, Standard 2
To use English to achieve academically in all content areas: Students will use English to obtain, process, construct, and provide subject matter information in spoken and **written** form.

TESOL then provides descriptors that can help teachers design assignments to reach Goal 2, Standard 2:

Descriptors

- comparing and contrasting information
- persuading, arguing, negotiating, evaluating, and justifying
- listening to, speaking, reading, and writing about subject matter information
- gathering information orally and in writing
- retelling information
- selecting, connecting, and explaining information
- analyzing, synthesizing, and inferring from information
- responding to the work of peers and others
- representing information visually and interpreting information presented visually
- hypothesizing and predicting
- formulating and asking questions
- understanding and producing technical vocabulary and text features according to content area
- demonstrating knowledge through application in a variety of contexts

Clearly, this standard and its descriptors can be used as a guide to designing writing assignments for second language writers. TESOL then provides indicators that show progress toward using English in spoken and written form:

Some Sample Progress Indicators for Goal 2, Standard 2

- compare and classify information using technical vocabulary
- synthesize, analyze, and evaluate information
- write a summary of a book, article, movie, or lecture
- locate information appropriate to an assignment in text or reference materials
- research information on academic topics from multiple sources
- take a position and support it orally or in writing
- define, compare, and classify objects
- read a story and represent the sequence of events (through pictures, words, music, or drama)
- locate reference material
- generate and ask questions of outside experts (e.g., about their jobs, experiences, interests, qualifications)
- gather and organize the appropriate materials needed to complete a task
- assess own written assignments
- edit and revise own written assignments

Source: www.tesol.org

Although some teachers may feel that standards narrow the curriculum, it is clear that the goals, standards, descriptors, and progress indicators are useful in guiding teachers as they develop courses and assignments. Even though the list is geared toward Grades 9–12, the items could certainly guide college instructors as well.

It is increasingly important for teachers to understand the underlying meaning of standards. When they are written, the progress indicators are actually components of assessment. Teachers are expected to assess their students to determine the level at which their students are able to perform a variety of specific skills. Currently, these standards and goals are used as a basis for both in-class and large-scale assessment. If teachers use the standards to guide classroom activities, they will not only be preparing students for standardized tests, but they will be providing authentic writing instruction as well. Ultimately, teachers need to answer this question: What do you want your students to be able to do as a result of instruction? From this starting point, teachers can create course materials and assessments to meet those goals.

Undoubtedly the sample progress indicators can be used to determine the goals of a writing class, a prerequisite in designing a course and its content. Write the goal. Attempt to distill it to one sentence. In a writing class, this goal could be translated into something like:

> In order to prepare for the writing students do at the university level, students will write essays in English in genres using rhetorical modes generally required by content area teachers: summary, comparison & contrast, and argument.

Following that, the descriptors and progress indicators on pages 60–61 can guide the creation of SWBATs (see Chapter 2 for a discussion of these), which leads to assignments and assessments for daily class meetings. As teachers develop their skills at creating goals, assignments, and assessments, they will begin to understand why the creation of each of these course components are part of one interconnected process.

Course catalog descriptions and class goals from two L2 writing courses at Wright State University, English 111 and English 112, are shown. The catalog course description of English 111:

> Designed for low-intermediate and intermediate-level ESL students who need work on the basics of sentence structure and paragraphing. This class is only offered fall quarter. Grades are pass/unsatisfactory.

Here is one teacher's interpretation of the catalog's course description, purpose, and goals for English 111:

English 111
English 111 is a course in written communication with emphasis on academic and professional writing. The purpose of the course is to help you become a better writer. In the process, you will learn how to identify your own strengths and weaknesses in writing, read critically, and increase your confidence in your own ability to write in a variety of situations. You will accomplish this by:
• Talking and listening—a lot—about writing processes, styles, and techniques • Reading—a lot—of the work of other writers • Writing—a lot—of your own material • Thinking—a lot—about your own work and others' work • Making mistakes—a lot of them—because we learn by taking risks and exploring possibilities

From Karen Hayes, Wright State ESL and first-year composition instructor

The catalog description of English 112:

> Designed for high-intermediate ESL students, this course is an introduction to the fundamentals of essay writing. It prepares students for the demands of college writing, emphasizing advanced sentence structure and style and organization and development of ideas for writing. Grades are pass/unsatisfactory.

Here is one teacher's interpretation of the catalog's course description, purpose, and goals for English 112:

English 112
Course description: This advance writing course will help you prepare for English 101/102 and other academic courses by improving your reading and writing skills.
GOALS: • Write two well-developed essays • Write timed essays in class on topics related to the class readings. • Improve sentence structure, style, organization. • Develop the ability to summarize. • Recognize and correct grammar errors.

From Julie Prugh, former Wright State University ESL writing instructor

Designing Assignment/Assessment Tasks for the Classroom

Once teachers define the purpose and goals of their courses, they can begin to create assignments that will help students meet those goals. Selecting items from the sample progress indicators can help shape assignments. For example, the progress indicator *comparing and contrasting information* can guide us in creating an assignment for a comparison/contrast essay. An assignment that asks students to compare and contrast two social networking sites—Facebook and MySpace—is shown on pages 65–67. The assignment includes a pre-writing worksheet and the actual assignment with criteria and the rubric for evaluation of the assignment.

The progress indicator *assess own written assignments* can guide us in creating a self-assessment assignment. An example of this type of assignment appears in Appendix 1.

A study of the assignments included so far reveals that the act of developing an assignment includes creating all portions of the assignment—the actual assignment, the criteria for that assignment, and the evaluation instrument for the assignment. Before teachers can create any assignment/assessment, they have to know what they want to know about what their students can do. *Every assignment is an assessment.* The act of assigning contains within it the essence of assessing. Moreover, every assignment should have its own unique criteria and rubric, and the rubric must clearly represent the criteria.

Timed Essays and Prompt Development

One of the most frequently used types of in-class assessment is the timed essay, even though the one-shot essay can be problematic for ESL teachers for a number of reasons. Leki reminds us: "As ESL teachers evaluate the writing of their students, the primary objectives should be long-term improvement and cognitive change" (as cited in Reid, 1993, p. 229). If positive

3RD WRITING ASSIGNMENT—PROS & CONS OF SOCIAL NETWORKING SITES

Pre-writing

What do you know about Facebook & MySpace?

How do you think these websites are used for communicating with friends and/or family?

Now, you will go to Facebook www.facebook.com/ & MySpace www.myspace.com/ with your partner(s). You are going to look at each site, and write some general information about each. Then, you are going to write some pros (positive points) of each site & cons (negative points of each site).

Social Networking Sites to Communicate with Friends and/or Family

Facebook®		**MySpace®**	
General Information: (Click on **"About"** at the bottom of the page)		General Information: (Click on **"About"** at the bottom of the page)	
Pros:	Cons:	Pros:	Cons:

Outline

Now, you will use the ideas in your chart to write an outline for your paragraph. Remember when you write an outline, you write the **main points** that you would like to include in your paragraph; you don't have to write down every idea. You should do this when you begin writing the 1st Draft.

Topic Sentence: ______________________________

____

General Information about Facebook & MySpace: ______________________________

____

____

____

Pros of Facebook: ______________________________

____

Cons of Facebook: ______________________________

____

Pros of MySpace: ______________________________

____

Cons of MySpace: ______________________________

____

Conclusion (Choose site that is the best for communicating with friends and/or family & explain why):

____

____

____

____

From Trisha Folck, Wright State University ESL writing instructor

3RD Writing Assignment—Analyzing Pros & Cons for Social Networking Sites

For your 3rd Writing Assignment, you will write a paragraph about the pros & cons of two social networking sites. You will evaluate Facebook & MySpace and decide which one is better for communicating with your friends and/or family.

Paragraph Evaluation

Criteria	Points
Organization: The paragraph begins with a topic sentence. Then it discusses pros and cons of both social networking sites and decides which one is better for keeping in touch with friends and/or family. Uses connectors to show relationship between ideas.	**/3**
Topic Sentence: Paragraph includes a clear topic sentence (main idea).	**/2**
Pros: Paragraph discusses pros (positive aspects) of both social networking sites. It includes enough details/examples to support ideas.	**/3**
Cons: Paragraph discusses cons (negative aspects) of both social networking sites. It includes details/examples to support ideas.	**/3**
Concluding Sentence(s): Paragraph discusses which social networking site is better for keeping in touch with friends and/or family.	**/3**
Vocabulary: Vocabulary is clear, specific, varied, and used correctly. Use different nouns, verbs, connectors, and adjectives throughout the paragraph.	**/2**
Grammar (Verbs): "Be" verb, simple present tense & present progressive tense are used correctly. Subjects and verbs agree.	**/2**
Grammar (Nouns, Articles & Quantifiers): Singular and plural nouns are used correctly. Articles (*a, an, the*) & Quantifiers (*some, any, many, much, a few, a little* & *a lot of*) are used correctly.	**/2**
Grammar (Connectors): Connectors (*and, but, so,* & *because*) are used correctly to connect ideas.	**/2**
Spelling & Mechanics: Most words are spelled correctly, punctuation is correct, and paragraph form is followed.	**/2**
Drafts: Includes outline, 1st, 2nd, 3rd, & Final Draft with corrections.	**/1**
Total:	**+ /25**

From Trisha Folck, Wright State University ESL writing instructor change is the goal, then the assignments teachers design should be those that allow comparisons of earlier examples of writing with writing done later in the term. This provides a tool for monitoring both improvement in writing and the maturation of the way students think about writing. Portfolios (discussed on pages 79–85) allow for these comparisons. However, timed essay tests are used to assess student knowledge in a variety of disciplines; therefore, timed essay tests will be discussed here.

The timed essay test begins with the *prompt,* or the task stimulus to which students are to respond. Creating explicit, nonambiguous prompts for writing tasks and timed essay exams can be a daunting task. These steps can help teachers produce good writing prompts for in-class essay exams and for writing assignments outside class.

Direction for Writing Prompts
State a context in one to two sentences. State the directions in a separate paragraph from the context. These should include format, audience, and topic. Define the mode of the essay using words such as *define, contrast, argue,* and *convince.*

A good prompt consists of all the information students need to develop an appropriate response to the assignment including context and directions that tell the writer the purpose for writing, the audience, and the format of the finished essay.

An example of a good prompt is shown:

CONTEXT
Many people think that students are not learning enough in school. They want to shorten school vacations and make students spend more of the year in school. Other people think that lengthening the school year and shortening vacations is a bad idea because students use their vacations to learn important things outside school.
DIRECTIONS
Write a letter (FORMAT) to the local school board (AUDIENCE) either in favor of or against (ASSERTION OPTIONS) lengthening the school year (TOPIC). Give specific reasons to support your opinion that will convince (MODE/PERSUASION) the school board to agree with you.

www.you-can-teach-writing.com/writing-prompts-functions.html

This prompt is excellent because it provides a context and defines the audience. The topic and the directions are clear. All the information students need to complete the assignment is included. Further, it is a topic that engages students because it has implications pertinent to their lives. White (1998) reminds us that writing ability will vary according to topic; better results are produced if the writer is interested in what she has to write about.

Improperly written prompts can elicit a uniform but unintended response, or students may respond with an unexpected variety of interpretations of the prompt. Poorly written prompts do not specify a context, the topic is vague, and the point of the assignment is missing. If we provide an audience for students in our writing assignments, we can help students to move to a more sophisticated level. Examples of ineffective writing prompts:

Examples of Improperly Written Prompts (all taken from essay tests at university level)
Indian armed resistance after 1760 was pointless. Discuss.
Discuss the use of metaphor in *To Kill a Mockingbird*.
Discuss the following: *The Prince of Tides* was neither about princes nor tides.

Imagine how these prompts might be interpreted by second language writers.

Like it or not, some teachers feel an obligation to prepare their students for essay tests. While the timed essay has been much maligned for its truncating of the writing process and its promotion of formulaic writing (the five-paragraph essay), many second language writers will be asked to draw on the skill of writing a timed essay. Taking the TOEFL®, the International English Language Testing System (IELTS), or the Test of English for International Communication (TOEIC®), writing for a test in sociology; taking proficiency tests in settings that are pre K–12 in the United States; and taking the new SAT timed writing test—these are just a few examples of occasions when students need the ability to produce clear, concise essays rapidly.

Criteria Generation

Best practices in second language writing assessment ask teachers to establish *criteria* for assignments. The criteria for any assignment should be clearly and briefly stated in language that students will understand, should be observable, and should include a statement of behavior. For instance, a teacher might assign a process essay. A process essay describes a process—baking cookies, washing the dog, painting a room—and begins with the first step in the process, proceeding in time through the last step in the process. In order to familiarize her students with the criteria for a process essay, the teacher might have her students read several process essays, guiding them through careful analysis of the readings, looking for what makes a process essay a process essay. Some of the questions students might think about while reading could include:

- What is the process in the paper?
- How many steps are there in the process?
- Why is each step important?

The teacher might then supply her students with a list of carefully crafted, detailed criteria on which they will be graded, or she may even ask her students to help in the creation of the criteria. She might tell her students that she will be looking for ways in which they delineate a process in their essay. If students do not understand the criteria, the teacher should elaborate. When students know what the criteria are, the result is enhanced uniformity of focus. It also gives the teacher greater ability to judge if students are able to perform the tasks being assessed. Once these criteria are established, they can guide the creation of a scoring rubric.

An example of an in-class writing assignment including the criteria for the assignment is shown on page 71. Notice that the prompts for the assignment are rather short but that the teacher has suggested reading material to contextualize the writing assignment. The teacher also provides carefully crafted criteria, this time with a focus on grammar issues that have been addressed in class.

Name: ______________________________ Total Points: /18

In-Class Paragraph # 5

1. In your reading class, you have started (or will soon start) to discuss aspects of the mass media. Today, you will write your in-class paragraph on this subject. Please read the following prompts:
   a. Write about your favorite television program. Say what kind of program it is, describe what it is about, and explain why you like it.
   b. Choose a recent news event that has received a lot of attention in the media. Describe the news event and explain why you think it has received so much attention.
   c. "Advertising is a necessary evil." Do you agree with this statement? Why or why not?
2. Write the letter of the prompt at the top of your paper. For example, "Topic A," etc.
3. **Skip lines!**
4. Your response should be about 1–1 ½ pages long.
5. After you write your response, edit your paper for the following issues that we have discussed in grammar class. Please do not rewrite your paragraph! I want to see your editing!

Criteria	Strong	Good	Adequate	Not Very Good	Weak
The paragraph uses a variety of relative clauses to describe nouns. Relative clauses have appropriate punctuation and are well-edited.	4	3.5	3	2.5	2–0
The paragraph has a variety of noun, verb, and adjective complements. Complements are appropriate and well-edited.	4	3.5	3	2.5	2–0
The paragraph uses the present time frame or the past time frame consistently. Shifts in verb tenses include time expressions that explain the shift.	4	3.5	3	2.5	2–0
The paragraph's sentence structure and grammatical complexity are appropriate for level 3.	3	2.5	2	1.5	1–0
The paragraph is well-edited for other grammatical problems that can interfere with the reader's understanding.	3	2.5	2	1.5	1–0

Comments:

From Sharon Tjaden-Glass, former Wright State University ESL writing instructor

Teachers can also engage students deeply in the classroom assessment process to better focus attention on students' own understanding of their growth and accomplishment. By asking students to reflect on their own language and composition abilities in these ways, teachers can foster more authentic assessment of student achievement and more engagement in the classroom.

Rubric Creation

The types of rubrics used to evaluate writing were discussed in Chapter 2, but creating them is one of the most worrisome and often overwhelming writing assessment. The best advice for teachers when considering creating a rubric is to adopt and adapt. O'Malley & Valdez-Pierce (1996), other second language writing scholars (Casanave, 2004; Ferris & Hedgcock, 2005; Reid, 1993), and other assessment scholars (Brown, 2004; Weigle, 2002) provide examples of rubrics immediately useful or as a basic guide for many purposes in and out of the classroom. The Internet also provides countless sites containing rubrics. See for example: Rubistar: (http://rubistar.4teachers.org/index.php) or TeacherVision: (www.teachervision.fen.com/teaching-methods-and-management/rubrics/4521.html).

While these sites do not specifically address second language writing, and although some do not allow teachers to enter their own criteria, these sites do provide excellent *starting points* and lists of criteria to consider when creating rubrics for many assignments.

However, even though these scoring guides are helpful, they still need to be adapted to the specific classroom situation for each teacher. Remembering that all assessment should be locally designed and locally controlled, adapting scoring rubrics (other than creating your own) is one way to ensure that the students you teach will be assessed on exactly what you have attempted to teach them rather than the opposite—teaching what will be tested. It is often very easy for us to design the test and then teach to it; however, this is backward pedagogy—the tail wagging the dog, so to speak. No Child Left Behind has permeated our national psyche so deeply that many believe testing can and should control all the myriad aspects at work in the classroom. However, we should work in the opposite direction; teachers and students should control the inner workings and intent of the classroom. Democratic classrooms should not be controlled from the outside (see Emery & Ohanian, 2004: Shannon, 2001); classroom control belongs in the hands of the stakeholders: the teachers and the students. There are many paths to building practical and functional scoring rubrics; however, all of them involve these five steps:

Steps to Creating Rubrics
• Develop the goals for your course and daily class meetings.
• Select the assessment tasks that provide data aligned with goals.
• Develop performance standards for each of these goals.
• Develop means for differentiation of performances (categories) based on well-described criteria.
• Rate (assign weight or value to) the categories (for analytical scoring) so that students understand their relative values.

Remember that the writing assessment process and the creation of the assignments, criteria, and rubrics are tremendously interconnected (Crusan, 2010). To be perfectly frank, if a teacher designs a good writing assignment, his criteria and grading method will be transparent to his students, although a list of the criteria and the actual rubric should most certainly be provided to the students. An assignment that carefully marries these components is shown on pages 74–76.

DESCRIPTION OF ESSAY # 2

For your second essay, you will write a research argument about one of these topics: the death penalty or the legalization of drugs. Your reading textbook has two articles that give a good description of these issues and tell you why some people support or oppose these issues. You can read about "The Death Penalty" on pages 177–179; you can read about "The War on Drugs" on pages 183–184.

> **What Is an Argument?**
>
> People don't always agree about issues. An argument shows the reader two sides of an issue about which people don't agree. For this assignment, your teacher has selected two possible topics for your paper along with two research questions. Writing an argument is difficult! Your teacher has given you these research questions and possible thesis statements to help get you started! This is still your paper because you will develop your ideas about the reasons for your thesis statement.

First, choose which topic interests you. Then, consider the research question for each of these topics:

Research Questions

1. Death Penalty: Since the death penalty does not decrease the number of crimes, should the death penalty be stopped in the United States?

   Possible Thesis Statements

   a. Yes

      The death penalty should be stopped in the United States because REASON 1 and REASON 2.

   b. No

      Although the death penalty does not decrease the number of crimes, it should still be used because REASON 1 and REASON 2.

2. Legalization of Drugs: Should recreational drugs be legalized in the United States?

   Possible Thesis Statements

   a. Yes

      Recreational drugs should be legalized in the United States because REASON 1 and REASON 2.

   b. No

      Recreational drugs should not be legalized in the United States because REASON 1 and REASON 2.

How Many Pages Should My Paper Have?

Your paper should contain a successful introduction, a clear thesis statement, two body paragraphs that explain your supporting reasons, one body paragraph that discusses the counterarguments of this position, and a clear conclusion. Your paper should be as long as it needs to be. A rubric for this paper is available on WebCT.

What Is a Counterargument?

A counterargument is a reason that the opposing side gives in support of its position. We will discuss this more as you do research.

Academic Research

For this paper, you will need to have **at least two sources** (articles, books, academic websites) that you quote or paraphrase in your paper. Remember that you should limit the number of quotations that you use. You should mostly use paraphrases. You should not use personal experience for this paper; instead, you should use academic research.

One of your sources can be your reading textbook, *Academic Encounters: Life in Society* (Cambridge University Press, 2002). Your second source should be one that you find through the library's search engine. On May 5th, our class will visit the library and a librarian will show you how to find good articles, books, and academic websites that you can use to support the ideas in your paper. **You may not use websites that you find independently through Yahoo, Google, or any other nonlibrary search engine. If you want to become a successful university student, you need to know how to use the library's search engine and find appropriate academic books and articles.**

Works Cited Page

A research paper needs to have a Works Cited page. This is a page at the end of your paper that lists the sources that you quoted, paraphrased, or summarized in your paper. In MLA style, this page is called Works Cited. In APA style, it is called References. Notice at the end of *Sourcework*, there are sample essays that have a final page called "References." (pages 210, 215, 221) However, we will learn MLA style in the class because this is the style that you will need to use in your first writing courses in college.

What is MLA style? On WebCT, there is a PDF file that explains MLA style and how to use it. It is under the icon "Writer's Reference." You should print this file and keep it to use the rest of the quarter. There are two files (pages 370–391, pages 392–412). Print them both!

From Sharon Tjaden-Glass, former Wright State University ESL writing instructor

Rubric for Essay # 2

Criteria	Excellent	Good	Okay	Not Good	Weak	Missing
Overall Goals						
The introduction engages the reader with interesting information or background information.	8	7	6	5	4	0
The thesis statement includes the topic, the position on the topic, and the two reasons that the writer supports the position.	8	7	6	5	4	0
The essay follows this organization: body paragraph 1 that discusses reason 1, body paragraph 2 that discusses reason 2, and body paragraph 3 that discusses counterarguments.	8	7	6	5	4	0
Each body paragraph begins with a topic sentence that identifies the main idea of the paragraph.	8	7	6	5	4	0
Each body paragraph provides relevant and reasonable examples, details, and research to support the topic sentence.	8	7	6	5	4	0
Counterarguments address reasons for the opposing position. The writer successfully refutes the counterargument.	8	7	6	5	4	0
The conclusion summarizes the main points of the essay and uses one of the conclusion strategies mentioned in the textbook.	8	7	6	5	4	0
The essay has significantly changed and improved from the first draft.	8	7	6	5	4	0
MLA Goals						
The essay includes in-text citations that are appropriately integrated with the student's writing and formatted according to the MLA guide. Citations are not "dumped" in the paper and sources are not plagiarized.	5	4	3	2	1	0
A Works Cited page is on a separate sheet of paper at the end of the essay and cites sources accurately and appropriately.	5	4	3	2	1	0
Other Goals						
The paper is accurately formatted, using Times New Roman, 12 point font, double spacing, and appropriate headings.	7	6	5	4	3	0
Guiding language is used throughout the essay to connect the points to the thesis and move the reader between ideas and paragraphs.	5	4	3	2	1	0
Subjects and verbs agree throughout the essay.	5	4	3	2	1	0
Verb tenses are used appropriately and consistently.	5	4	3	2	1	0
Word choice and word forms are appropriate.	5	4	3	2	1	0
Punctuation is used well; there are few problems with comma splices, run-ons, and fragments.	5	4	3	2	1	0
The grammar is comprehensible.	7	6	5	4	3	0

Grading Scale: A = 101–113 B = 90–100 C = 79–89 D = 68–78 F = below 68

Comments:

From Sharon Tjaden-Glass, former Wright State University ESL writing instructor

Peer Review and Its Place in Writing Assessment

Peer assessment is another powerful tool once students are taught how to apply performance standards to the work of others. Possible questions students can be asked to answer about a peer's writing include:

- What did you like about the paper?
- What facts or ideas could be added to the paper?
- What changes could be made to improve the paper?

Of course, more focused questions can be aligned to the specific assignment criteria and the rubric that will be used for its evaluation. An example of a peer review exercise is shown on page 78.

Liu & Hansen (2002) point out the cognitive, social, linguistic, and practical benefits to peer response. Cognitive issues include such notions as building critical-thinking skills and audience awareness. Peer response also allows for the "establishment of collegial ties and friendship" (social), "language skill practice and finding the right words to express ideas" (linguistic), and "reinforcement of process writing and time efficiency" (practical) (p. 8). According to educators, some benefits to peer assessment are:

Benefits of Peer Review
• Provides a wider audience for student writers • Offers students the opportunity to receive feedback on the strengths and weaknesses of their writing • Teaches students to critically analyze their own writing and the writing of others • Motivates multiple drafts and substantial revisions • Familiarizes students with the format, style, criteria, and expectations of writing in the discipline studied • Promotes active learning • Builds classroom community • Models the interpersonal, interactive, and group problem-solving nature of most workplace writing • Reduces the teacher's feedback workload

www.mwp.hawaii.edu/resources/peer_review.htm

PEER REVIEW SHEET
Answer these questions as you read the paper. Avoid one-word responses (yes, no, etc.).
Writer:
Paper Title:
Evaluator:
• What are the strengths of the paper? What about the paper works well?
• Does the title fit the essay? Why or why not? Suggestions?
• Does the introduction grab the reader's attention? Why or why not? Suggestions?
• What is the author's thesis? Does the paper support the thesis? Explain.
• Is the draft effectively organized? Could it be organized differently? Suggestions?
• Are the paragraphs unified? Are there clear topic sentences? Does every sentence in the paragraph support the topic sentence? Are there clear, effective transitions? Suggestions?
• Is the conclusion effective? Does it adequately conclude the essay? Suggestions?
• Where would the paper benefit from additional support and examples?
• Does the author appropriately address the audience? Why or why not? Suggestions?
• Make two suggestions for the next draft.

Portfolio Assessment

In a process-oriented writing classroom, portfolio assessment fits well, as it clearly shows that writing is a process (White, 1998). All of the writing classes at my institution, both L1 and L2, rely on the portfolio as the largest component of the course. The portfolio is valuable because it tracks growth over time. However, White (1998) claims, "Portfolios pose problems for assessment because of their sheer bulk and the uncontrolled conditions under which they are produced" (p. 120). Therefore, it is of utmost importance that teachers make the specifications for the portfolio known early on in the course, preferably on the syllabus at the beginning of the course, once again making assessment transparent. Directions can read as follows:

> In your final portfolio due on the last day of class, you will include your best copies of our two essays, your final piece of timed writing, and your own assessment of your progress in this class. Other assignments may also be needed, so be sure that you keep all of the assignments you write for this class.

Portfolios appear to mirror the writing process because they:

- Provide collections of student writing, addressing the problem of overgeneralizing from single writing samples.
- Include writing produced in natural settings rather than under artificial test conditions.
- Reflect an ongoing curriculum.
- Document students' drafting and revising processes.
- Include students' reflections on their writing.

Murphy & Grant, 1996, p. 289

Assessing portfolios can be done in a variety of ways, but the work of assessment is spread out over an entire term rather than at the end of the course. Teachers in a portfolio-based class require multiple drafts and writing conferences at which they provide feedback on drafts in progress. However, a final grade must be attached to the portfolios, so I have included one rubric designed around the portfolio process at my institution (see pages 81–84).

Are portfolios the answer to classroom writing assessment? Callahan (1995) suggests that "healthy portfolio projects are highly contextualized, have clearly defined purposes, are carefully designed to meet those purposes, are understood and supported by all who are involved, and are always open to revision" (p. 143). On the other hand, O'Neill, Moore, & Huot (2009) present a different perspective. They claim that "if the teachers conceptualize and present portfolio assessment differently from each other (and from the program's intentions), then students will have different conceptions and experiences with it, and this experience may not be what is intended" (p. 107). And in reality, some portfolios can be artificial. For instance, if portfolios include only students' best work, are they truly a reflection of growth over time?

Whatever way teachers choose to assess their L2 writers' work, these points are important to keep in mind and will produce effective assessment procedures. These points, by now, might sound rather redundant, but they will aid in cementing the definition of good writing assessment:

- Teachers should always identify the purpose of the assessment and the learning that is to be assessed.
- Teachers should select assessment instruments and procedures that match learning goals.
- Teachers should gather multiple evaluations to present a more complete picture of what students have learned and share these pictures with their learners.

Portfolio Rubric

Name ____________		
Final Portfolio		
	Points	Grade
Portfolio Contents (25)		
Final Essay Exam (250)		
Self-Assessment Letter (225)		
Compare/Contrast (250)		
Cause/Effect (250)		
Total (1000)		
Portfolio Contents and Organization	(a point for each check)	
	Present	Labeled
Left Pocket		
-Final Essay Exam		
-2nd Practice Essay		
-1st Practice Essay		
-Compare/Contrast #3		
-Compare/Contrast #2		
-Compare/Contrast #1		
-Cause/Effect #3		
-Cause/Effect #2		
-Cause/Effect #1		
	Present	MLA
Right Pocket		
-Self-Assessment Letter		
-Compare/Contrast		
-Cause/Effect		
The portfolio has an overall nice presentation.		
The portfolio is organized.		
Total		

Final Essay Exam								
x	**Content**							Points
5	Responds to question or prompt appropriately	5	4	3	2	1	0	
3	Uses an introduction strategy (or combination of various ones)	5	4	3	2	1	0	
3	Uses a concluding strategy (or combination of various ones)	5	4	3	2	1	0	
3	Has thesis that conveys cause/effect organization	5	4	3	2	1	0	
3	Uses multiple paragraphs to successfully support a thesis	5	4	3	2	1	0	
3	Uses specifc details and examples from personal knowledge	5	4	3	2	1	0	
	Organization							
3	Uses appropriate cause/effect organization (as discussed in class)	5	4	3	2	1	0	
2	Uses transitions and other logical connectors appropriately	5	4	3	2	1	0	
3	Has a clear introduction, body, and conclusion	5	4	3	2	1	0	
2	Has a clear thesis statement that's easy to find (at end of intro)	5	4	3	2	1	0	
3	Has a thesis statement with a topic and controlling idea	5	4	3	2	1	0	
2	Includes clear topic, supporting, and concluding sentences	5	4	3	2	1	0	
	Grammar							
3	Has only minor errors in subject-verb agreement, verb tense, and form	5	4	3	2	1	0	
3	Avoids run-ons and fragments	5	4	3	2	1	0	
2	Shows knowledge of spelling and punctuation rules	5	4	3	2	1	0	
2	Uses a variety of sentence structures (complex, simple, compound)	5	4	3	2	1	0	
	Vocabulary							
2	Uses a range of varied vocabulary	5	4	3	2	1	0	
3	Has appropriate word choice and form that does not affect meaning	5	4	3	2	1	0	
				Total				
								/250
				Grade				
Self-Assessment Letter								

x	**Format**							
1	-In letter format (addressed "Dear Sarah," signed, etc.)	5	4	3	2	1	0	
2	-2–4 pages long	5	4	3	2	1	0	
1	-Typed and double-spaced	5	4	3	2	1	0	
	Content							
2	-Introduces each of the assignments	5	4	3	2	1	0	
2	-Tells what each assignment was and what the student wrote about	5	4	3	2	1	0	
4	-Talks about strengths of each of the essays	5	4	3	2	1	0	
4	-Talks about weaknesses of each of the essays	5	4	3	2	1	0	
3	-Discusses other aspects (work habits, participation, etc.)	5	4	3	2	1	0	
5	-Explains how all objectives for the class were met	5	4	3	2	1	0	
3	-Uses examples to support all of the above	5	4	3	2	1	0	
2	-Concludes with summary of work for the class and grade deserved	5	4	3	2	1	0	
3	-Explains why he/she is ready for English 101	5	4	3	2	1	0	
	Grammar, Vocabulary, and Mechanics							
3	-Avoids run-ons and fragments	5	4	3	2	1	0	
3	-All sentences clear (in meaning)	5	4	3	2	1	0	
3	-Uses proper verb tenses/forms	5	4	3	2	1	0	
2	-Uses proper word choice/form	5	4	3	2	1	0	
2	-Shows knowledge of punctuation and spelling system	5	4	3	2	1	0	
					Total			
								/225
					Grade			

Compare/Contrast								
x	**Content**							Points
3	Shows an understanding of assignment, follows directions	5	4	3	2	1	0	
3	Uses an introduction strategy (or combination of various ones)	5	4	3	2	1	0	
3	Uses a concluding strategy (or combination of various ones)	5	4	3	2	1	0	
3	Has thesis that conveys compare/contrast organization	5	4	3	2	1	0	
3	Uses multiple paragraphs to successfully support a thesis	5	4	3	2	1	0	
3	Uses specifc details and examples from personal knowledge	5	4	3	2	1	0	
	Organization							
3	Uses appropriate compare/contrast organization	5	4	3	2	1	0	
2	Uses transitions and other logical connectors appropriately	5	4	3	2	1	0	
3	Has a clear introduction, body, and conclusion	5	4	3	2	1	0	
2	Has a clear thesis statement that's easy to find (at end of intro)	5	4	3	2	1	0	
3	Has a thesis statement with a topic and controlling idea	5	4	3	2	1	0	
2	Includes clear topic, supporting, and concluding sentences	5	4	3	2	1	0	
	Grammar							
3	Has only minor errors in subject-verb agreement, verb tense, and form	5	4	3	2	1	0	
3	Avoids run-ons and fragments	5	4	3	2	1	0	
2	Shows knowledge of spelling and punctuation rules	5	4	3	2	1	0	
2	Uses a variety of sentence structures (complex, simple, compound)	5	4	3	2	1	0	
	Vocabulary							
2	Uses a range of varied vocabulary	5	4	3	2	1	0	
3	Has appropriate word choice and form that does not affect meaning	5	4	3	2	1	0	
	Format							
2	MLA format—double spaced, typed, appropriate headers, page #s, etc.	5	4	3	2	1	0	
				Total				
								/250
				Grade				

Cause/Effect								
x	**Content**							Points
3	Shows an understanding of assignment, follows directions	5	4	3	2	1	0	
3	Uses an introduction strategy (or combination of various ones)	5	4	3	2	1	0	
3	Uses a concluding strategy (or combination of various ones)	5	4	3	2	1	0	
3	Has thesis that conveys cause/effect organization	5	4	3	2	1	0	
3	Uses multiple paragraphs to successfully support a thesis	5	4	3	2	1	0	
3	Uses specifc details and examples from personal knowledge	5	4	3	2	1	0	
	Organization							
3	Uses appropriate cause/effect organization	5	4	3	2	1	0	
2	Uses transitions and other logical connectors appropriately	5	4	3	2	1	0	
3	Has a clear introduction, body, and conclusion	5	4	3	2	1	0	
2	Has a clear thesis statement that's easy to find (at end of intro)	5	4	3	2	1	0	
3	Has a thesis statement with a topic and controlling idea	5	4	3	2	1	0	
2	Includes clear topic, supporting, and concluding sentences	5	4	3	2	1	0	
	Grammar							
3	Has only minor errors in subject-verb agreement, verb tense, and form	5	4	3	2	1	0	
3	Avoids run-ons and fragments	5	4	3	2	1	0	
2	Shows knowledge of spelling and punctuation rules	5	4	3	2	1	0	
2	Uses a variety of sentence structures (complex, simple, compound)	5	4	3	2	1	0	
	Vocabulary							
2	Uses a range of varied vocabulary	5	4	3	2	1	0	
3	Has appropriate word choice and form that does not affect meaning	5	4	3	2	1	0	
	Format							
2	MLA format—double spaced, typed, appropriate headers, page #s, etc.	5	4	3	2	1	0	
				Total				
								/250
				Grade				

Suggestions for Teachers

Here's one way (there are many) to create a rubric. Try it yourself.

1. Choose one of your writing assignments.
2. List the criteria—what do you want your students to do in this paper? What must be included?
3. How will you grade the paper? What "counts"? How many total points are available?
4. Create descriptors. 5 could be stupendous (or excellent); 1 could be very poor (or marginal or working hard).
5. Share it with your students. Ask for their input about its fairness. Ask what they would add. Omit.
6. Try out some rubric makers from the Internet. Analyze their usefulness in terms of time and ease. Can teachers tailor the rubrics to fit their own assignments?

Chapter 4

Biases in Writing Assessment: What Are They and What Can We Do about Them?

> *Think of bias as a learned or emotional predisposition to believe a certain way, regardless of the facts. That's why bias is so tough to overcome. It weighs heavily on a person's thinking and warps it accordingly. So one usually is unaware of one's biases.*
>
> —Marilyn vos Savant

It is extremely difficult to develop any test without introducing cultural bias. A test is biased if members of one particular gender, culture, age group, language group, or race achieves statistically different results from the general population in any portion of the test. Lee, Breland, & Muraki (2004) acknowledged the importance of examining bias in writing prompts. They see significant cultural bias in writing prompts as having the ability to distort the meaning of essay scores for different cultural groups. This in turn could threaten test score validity.

In a discussion of test bias, Brown (2004) cites this prompt from IELTS to illustrate bias in writing assessment:

> You rent a house through an agency. The heating system has stopped working. You phoned the agency a week ago, but it has still not been mended. Write a letter to the agency. Explain the situation and tell them what you want them to do about it.

Brown finds the prompt authentic; that is, the notion that one might have to write a letter of complaint is highly probable. However, he sees cultural and economic assumption in the prompt. Will every student reading this prompt understand *rent*? What about *heating system*? Will every student understand the term *phoned*?

It is quite easy to become entangled in bias. One clear example is our tendency to think that our familiar technology is available to everyone. Imagine this homework assignment:

> *Go to Google, and search for reasons families should take a summer vacation.*

Inherent in these seemingly straightforward 13 words are several major but not necessarily obvious assumptions: that families have access to a computer in their home; that students have access to the Internet; that students understand how the term *go* is used in the sentence; that students understand Google; that students have the economic means to take a vacation; and that students can relate to being brought up in a family.

This chapter explores biases inherent in assessment in general and writing assessment in particular. In referring to such biases, it is important to point out that I am not using *bias* as a pejorative term; by *bias,* I simply mean individual-agenda, or discipline-based preference. Chief among these are teacher bias, peer bias, administrative bias, and political bias. These biases can be reflected in defining good writing, which creates problems for all students, but especially for L2 writers. These problems may stem from the often unarticulated competing agendas of standardized testing and classroom writing assessment or from various definitions of good writing as used in specific professions. These expectations are often unclear to students and other stakeholders. In addition to defining and exploring some implications of these biases, this chapter offers guidelines, strategies, and activities useful for helping L2 writers and L2 writing teachers understand discipline-specific writing requirements.

Teacher Bias

Writing assessment has persistently been an issue fraught with contention. Psychometricians retain and use both overt and covert biases, which colors beliefs about the best ways to assess writing, but they do not have a monopoly on bias. When it comes to writing and writing assessment, teachers are equally quick to express their opinions. All teachers, consciously or unconsciously, hold biases about virtually every aspect of the workings of their classrooms. At the beginning of the quarter of an assessment class, one of my students, who was teaching an L2 writing class at the time, was quite vocal about her aversion to using rubrics to assess student writing. However, after careful reading of the assigned material and participation in class discussions with me and with her peers, she tried some of the techniques in her writing class and gradually came to see that having carefully articulated assessment criteria made her a better teacher and assessor of her students' writing. She caught on to the importance and implications of "It depends!" (Johnson, 1999). It is critical to remember that the way we assess our students speaks volumes, identifying our purposes and articulating our principles more clearly than any mission statement ever could (White, Lutz, & Kamusikiri, 1996). In other words, actions speak louder than words

In an effort to examine biases to determine teachers' expectations of their students, one faculty task force (Intersegmental Committee of the Academic Senates of the California Community Colleges, the California State Universities, and the University of California 2002) conducted an Internet-based interview study designed to discover and analyze the degree of academic literacy that faculty expected of students entering California's public colleges and universities. The task force invited faculty from many disciplines who regularly teach introductory or first-year courses to answer questions regarding their expectations of students' reading, writing, and critical thinking. The survey, which uncovered a spectrum of *teacher beliefs, practices,* and *opinions* relating to writing patterns and teacher biases, included these findings:

- Faculty believe that only one-third of entering college students are sufficiently prepared for the two most frequently assigned writing tasks: analyzing information and arguments and synthesizing information from several sources.
- Faculty state that more than 50 percent of their students fail to produce papers relatively free of language errors.
- Faculty's judgments of students' ability emphasize thinking clearly, accurately, and compellingly through their writing. Faculty look for evidence in papers that students are stretching their minds and representing others' ideas responsibly.
- Faculty often ask students to complete complex writing tasks across the disciplines but provide little instruction or criteria for assessment.
- Faculty expect students to reexamine their thesis, to consider and reconsider additional points or arguments, to reshape and reconstruct as they compose, and to submit carefully revised and edited work.
- Faculty assign writing to ascertain how students think, to help students engage critically and thoughtfully with course readings, to demonstrate what students understand from lectures, to structure and guide their inquiry, to encourage independent thinking, and to invite them into the ongoing intellectual dialogue that characterizes higher education. (pp. 10–11)

Many respondents in this survey also expected that: writing instruction be part of every course taken in the last two years of high school; that the writing assignments given demand analysis, synthesis, and research; that students use texts for idea generation in addition to experiential writing; and that students be required to improve revision, editing, and proofreading skills.

How might the results of this survey be connected to biases in terms of L2 writing assessment? Clearly, teachers' biases, opinions, and expectations will affect their assessment of writing. This is particularly critical for L2 writing, which, like the writing of so-called "basic" writers, might be the writing least likely to fit the criteria, practices, and expectations mentioned. Those types of biases present problems for L2 writers because the practices, beliefs, and opinions often do not reflect what SLA researchers know about language acquisition—that it is a very gradual process. Plus, as we know, L2 writers' needs are often different from those of L1 writers. Ferris (2002) reminds us that L2 writers need "[more of a] focus on different linguistic issues or error patterns than native speakers do; feedback or error correction that is tailored to their linguistic knowledge or experience; and instruction that is sensitive to their unique linguistic deficits and needs for strategy training" (p. 5).

Teachers' (Assessors') Personality Types

When it comes to writing and what is good writing, people involved are not reluctant to express their preferences. For the purposes in this chapter, the people in a position to perform writing assessment might be divided into three basic (and possibly simplistic) categories:

Basic Personality Approaches to Assessment
Left-brain assessors: focus more on mechanical aspects of testing and rating and emphasize the logical continuity of thought and mechanical aspects of writing.
Right-brain assessors: place a high value on creative processes and the use of novel ideas, imagery, and poetic construction.
Whole-brain assessors: can use the left and right halves of the brain simultaneously, incorporating not only the technical but also the creative, giving appropriate weight to the mechanical and creative concurrently.

Assuming these three types of individual raters are influenced by their biases, they will use differing criteria to rate a paper, resulting in different feedback and grades.

Some teachers show a bias toward one form of assessment and use that form to the exclusion of all others. For example, I once worked with an educational psychology professor at a community college who believed that a teacher could assess anything with a multiple choice test. Her pedagogy and lock-step curriculum reflected this belief; her students ingested the required readings and class lectures and regurgitated answers on multiple choice instruments on a regular basis. Sadly, because her pedagogy encouraged only rote memorization and lacked reflective practice, most students left her class with little more than surface awareness of the principles of educational psychology and acquired very few tools to apply to their own pedagogy.

Bias Regarding Pedagogy

Certainly, the composition field has long been aware of the importance of the processes involved in writing. Emig (1971) studied the composing processes of a group of 12th graders and discovered that writing is much more than product; it is a nonlinear, exploratory, and generative process through which writers conceive, develop, and reformulate their ideas as they attempt to approximate meaning. Britton, Burgess, Martin, McLeod, & Rosen (1975) reiterated the importance of focus on process, calling for a close examination of what happens when a person writes. The subsequent research "both identified the complex nature of the composing process and raised questions about past approaches to the teaching of writing" (Zamel, 1982, p. 195). If writing is more than the final product, it stands to reason that we must assess the process through which writers negotiate in developing and articulating the final product. However, many teachers trained in current-traditional writing pedagogy might yet cling to these assumptions as the basis for their views regarding assessment. (This 18th-century rhetoric, emphasizing style, correctness, and concrete detail, while seemingly incomplete, narrow, and outdated, is very often the pedagogy used in composition classes.)

Many other teachers may be biased in one way or another depending on their personal definition of "good writing." Let's look at it this way: Good writing is, by definition, contextual. Medicine is a context; business is a context; liberal arts is a context. Between and often within each of these contexts, the definition of what constitutes "good writing" varies widely. This is not to suggest that these differences are bad; the point here lies with raising teacher and student awareness that fundamental differences exist.

Teachers' pedagogies clearly represent their preferences regarding assessment (Johnson, 1999). Berlin (1987) defined current-traditional rhetoric as a positivistic theory of composition with a concentration on correctness. In terms of writing, composition specialists have long suspected that many teachers, although they publicly eschew a focus on the final product of writing and celebrate process-centered writing instruction as excellent pedagogy, still practice current-traditional rhetoric in the classroom (Crowley, 1990). See Matsuda (2003a) for an in-depth discussion of current-traditional rhetoric.

In a survey designed to examine the definitions of effective discourse at Wright State University, I asked faculty why they require writing in their classes (Crusan, 2001):

Professors in the Study Require Writing Because Writing

- offers evidence of student understanding of the lesson.
- is a means by which we think and learn.
- is a powerful means of self-discovery and a radical agent for change.
- is the best way to express oneself.
- is an extension of critical thinking.
- allows for reflection on the course material.
- develops correlational skills.
- it is an important job skill.

Additionally, I found that the definition of good writing differs greatly from department to department. Moreover, many faculty share assumptions of current-traditional rhetoric's penchant for product over process. For instance, medical faculty members repeatedly stated that grammatical correctness was one of the most important features of good writing. On the other hand, music department faculty members consistently cited creativity, flow, and similar concepts—elements common to the structure of music. Some English department faculty mentioned content, genre, audience, purpose, and coherence as most meaningful and important. However, several literature specialists in the English department and teachers in other content areas in the liberal arts, such as modern languages, history, and political science, often seemed preoccupied with mechanical and grammatical issues to the exclusion of content. Business faculty repeatedly emphasized the importance of the short memo, or the even more concise bulleted list; consistently, business faculty stated that writing should be clear and succinct, almost terse, whenever possible. Key representations of qualities faculty cited as necessary for good writing are encapsulated in the boxes (Crusan, 2001).

Medicine, Science, Applied Sciences

- uses minimum words to express an idea (medicine)
- is focused on grammar, grammar, grammar (medicine)
- is grounded in an absence of ambiguity (physics)
- is accurate for fact-based prose (biology)
- uses vocabulary correctly (nursing)
- is large enough to cover the subject; short enough to be interesting (chemistry)
- has a strategy (psychology)
- uses key words, parallelism (medicine)

Liberal Arts

- eliminates slang (theatre)
- is legible and neat (music)
- has flow and rhythm that makes it enjoyable to read (music)
- uses varied sentence structure (art)
- uses analysis (political science)
- has passion (modern languages)
- uses transitions effectively; conclusions are effective (modern languages)

Business

- is brief and always to the point (management)
- instills confidence in the content
- is concise

Education

- "I believe 'good' is the lowest form of writing acceptable and for my students it must be factual, devoid of emotion, and thorough."
- cites often; uses quotes rarely
- uses language that the audience understands

Clearly, vast, field-specific differences of the definition of "good writing" exist. For example, some scientific articles are very brief summaries of study results. In other fields, however, articles are much longer with heavy reviews of the literature. In some essays, data are largely anecdotal, while other essays are written quantitatively, containing several distinct and discipline-specific components with numerical and statistical data in tables.

But what is most important in this discussion of the definitions of "good writing" remains the same—together, teachers and students can learn what characterizes good writing in a variety of disciplines, and teachers can aid in the emulation of that kind of writing. They can do this by investigating along with their students, the elements of good writing in a variety of disciplines. Of course, this type of pedagogical approach exposes our assumption that writing is static (Matsuda, 1997). In fact, Matsuda (2002) argues that "the goal of writing instruction has been construed as helping students to create texts that are unmarked in the eyes of the native speakers of certain varieties of English" (p. 193).

This same pedagogical approach also uncovers another assumption—that teachers as assessors of writing are consistent. Leki (1995) found otherwise when she asked ESL students, writing teachers, and content area teachers to rank four pieces of ESL writing. Her results showed vastly different ideas of the definition of good writing and the criteria by which writing should be judged. Leki claimed that English departments are "uniquely obligated to learn more about the many academic discourse villages around us, to develop awareness of what other faculty on our campuses are assuming about writing, and to use our expertise to support our colleagues' conscious examination of their diverse criteria for high-quality writing" (p. 45).

The various definitions of "good writing" create problems especially for L2 writers. L2 writing teachers need to stress to their students that not only do differences exist when writing in a specific language, but also when writing for a specific audience within that language or even a specific instructor within a discipline, as shown in Crusan 2001. All writers, including L2 writers, will be evaluated differently depending on their audience. What represents good writing in one discipline may not represent good writing in another. For example, good writing in business is often reduced to a series of bullet points, while good writing in an L2 composition class might be in the form of an argmentative essay. If teachers do not make the existence of difference (bias) explicit to their students, they are complicit in their students' failures. This problem looms large, especially at the university level, but it can also occur in other contexts where there is neither agreement on what constitutes good writing nor a priori knowledge on how a particular type of writing will be assessed. As an L2 writer herself, Li (1995) mused, "It is the life in both worlds (second language learner and doctoral student at an American university) which opened my eyes to the situatedness of 'good writing,' and it is the pluralistic American culture and the 'free-wheeling' discussions in graduate seminars in an American university that broadened my vision to see the deep-seated arbitrariness of all standards and to question the fairness of their enforcement" (p. xiii). These differences, difficult for a preeminent graduate student, now well-known scholar, might be nearly impossible to understand and negotiate for not-so-motivated undergraduate L2 writers.

L2 writing teachers might use these strategies to raise student awareness of difference in the definitions of "good writing" and address the arbitrariness of those definitions:

- invite guest speakers from various departments and professions into L2 writing classrooms.
- examine different genres of writing—poetry, business letter and memos, book reviews, academic essays, press releases.
- ask students to list what they perceive good writing to be.
- assign a research project wherein students investigate through interviews what other teachers think about good writing and writing assessment.
- help students construct emails to be sent to experts in different fields (either academic or popular or both) with questions about their writing processes and their views of writing assessment.

In addition to raising student awareness of differences in the definitions of good writing, teachers need to make students aware of another factor as well—just as there may be inconsistency in the definition of good writing from one site to the next, there may well be inconsistency in writing assessment methods as well. For example, in a history class essay test, a student might be assessed primarily on demonstration of content knowledge of the subject, as well as the more mechanical aspects of writing. When it comes to mechanics, though, the history professor might assess an L2 writer more harshly, because she may not be as aware as L2 professionals of the gradual acquisition of both the productive and receptive skills of language. So might she unfairly assess the student's knowledge. According to Ferris (2002), "Both anecdotal and research evidence suggests that at least in some settings, university professors and employees find ESL errors distracting and stigmatizing" (p. 9). Often, an L2 writer will have great difficulty ever producing a "perfect" paper, especially concerning the mechanical aspects of writing; in fact, this is a difficult task for a native speaker of any language. One option is for teachers to encourage the use of editors and proofreaders to craft papers as error-free as possible. Specifically, L2 writing teachers may consider requiring students to use the writing center or private tutors. If the writing represents a high-stakes outcome, as in writing for publication, then additional editorial input may spell the difference between acceptance and rejection of that paper, which in turn has profound ramifications on the writer's career.

Bias toward Grammar Correctness

It is an unfortunate truth that some teachers may harshly and severely downgrade a student's product when that student repeats an error in a subsequent paper. For instance, a student might commit comma splice errors in a first paper. The teacher may warn the student regarding the error, with or without any kind of instruction; possibly the teacher's instructions and criteria will not be as explicit as the L2 writer might need. If in a subsequent paper the student makes a similar mistake, the student might receive very harsh criticism and a lowering of the paper grade or a term grade based almost entirely on the mechanical aspects of the paper.

This narrow focus on the aspects of punctuation and mechanics is problematic for several reasons. First language (L1) acquisition research (Freeman & Freeman, 2004) clearly indicates that any kind of language acquisition/teaching takes quite a long time to become incorporated into a person's cognitive processes. Even a person writing in her first language has difficulty remembering and incorporating rules of punctuation; writing is much more than "oral language written down," and some scholars (Bergmann, Hall, & Ross, 2007; Freeman & Freeman, 2004) contend that we learn writing consciously rather than acquiring it naturally. Further, writing is always about juggling multiple concerns of discourse, and as one is focusing on improving abilities in one area, the other areas tend to decline (Carroll, 2003). For a teacher to treat error (and the writer) so severely indicates a lack of understanding of the basic tenets of language acquisition and demonstrates a clear bias toward the mechanical aspects of writing.

For an example, let's consider one teacher who had a pet peeve (bias) about a grammatical construction in English. In their high school years, my children had an English teacher who loathed the passive voice. Before she would read a student's paper, she would scrutinize the work and deduct one-half point for every instance of passive voice in the paper. She believed that passive voice should be eradicated from her students' writing. Of course, she informed the students of her distaste for the passive voice and enumerated ways to avoid the offending formation, but the level of her students' understanding is another question. Often I would sit with my children as they were working on their papers. I would help them locate and identify passive construction in their writing, remind them that their teacher found it offensive, and encourage them to rework the sentences. Even with this help and consistent warnings from their teacher, I found numerous instances of the passive voice in subsequent papers. When I reflect on this, I am not even sure that my children understood the rules or the logic of passive voice. However, I am certain that my children developed a dislike for writing and began to doubt their writing abilities. As I have reflected on these experiences with my children and their writing, I have often thought that their experiences were a clear demonstration that the writing skills of students evolve incrementally. The development of writing skills seems to depend on the students' levels of cognition, their ability to process the information, and often their level of motivation. For my children, whom I had always considered very good writers, writing in their native language (especially for this teacher) posed a major problem—might it be as difficult for the L2 writer? Or might it be even more difficult?

This visceral and very prescriptive reaction of certain teachers to a specific mechanical aspect of writing may be due to unanalyzed internalization; in other words, the teacher may have been harshly criticized for the same error, so much so that a conditioned response occurred whenever the particular grammatical construction appears. For instance, often in the late 1950s and early 1960s, students were taught that a comma should never be used before the last item in a series. Teachers told writers to omit the final comma, citing its redundancy. However, usage manuals from that era (Hacker, 2003; Harris, 1999; Ruszkiewicz, Hairston, & Seward, 2001) stated "the comma after the last item before *and* or *or* is preferred, but it may be omitted *if there is no possibility of misreading*" (emphasis added) (Harris, p. 134). Further, Hacker (2003) cautions us to "be aware that its (the comma's) omission can result in ambiguity or misreading" (p. 237). Clearly then, unexamined, unreflective teaching coupled with a lack of understanding that language changes can impact students negatively. It is important that teachers realize the dynamic evolutionary aspects of language so that we do not so easily promulgate possibly outmoded styles or personal preferences through generations of teachers and students.

I contend that some teachers have little idea about (or have given little thought to) the processes, both conscious and unconscious, that they move through to produce a piece of writing, even if they consider themselves writers. It is also quite possible that they have minimal training in the teaching of writing or, for whatever reason, have been unaware of or unable to access current research on composition pedagogy. Unfortunately, teachers who focus primarily on mechanical aspects often instill fear (of writing) in students, resulting in students obsessing about their writing. Grammar police haunt them and cause them to question: "Are the commas in the right places? Are the words spelled correctly? Are there verb tense errors?" Students' main focus is diverted to avoiding mechanical errors at all costs, errors that might best be addressed during the revision and editing stages. Instead, in an effort to avoid error, the L2 writer risks little and may produce work that contains simplistic language, syntax, and ideas.

What might a teacher do to avoid instilling fear into her writing students and instead help them to become risk-takers with language, writers who make meaning through writing and thereby possess more understanding of themselves as writers and thinkers? Although writing assessment will never be perfect and no one method will be the balm to soothe all teachers' assessment woes, there is one assessment principle that may prevent undue stress for students and possibly rectify teacher bias. Valdez-Pierce (2000) maintains that we should never construct an assignment without also constructing the means of assessing the assignment. Additionally, the assessment criteria should be fronted (Ferris & Hedgcock, 2005; Valdez-Pierce, 2000) so that students are constantly aware of the criteria on which they will be evaluated. To avoid assessments filled with innate biases, we should work to make our assessment criteria as authentic and congruent with theory as possible.

In an effort to discover what works for their students, Crusan & Cornett (2002) conducted a longitudinal study of L2 writers. In the classes they taught, they found that students experienced frustration with the seemingly arbitrary assessment of their work. Consequently, the researchers set about to raise their students' awareness of the criteria by which their writing would be judged. They also taught their students some of the language of assessment—namely, the language and logic of the rubrics by which they would be evaluated. Further, students practiced assessing their own and their peers' writing using assignment rubrics. Because of these classroom practices, students' confidence increased as their understanding of the logic linking their writing scores with what they had written increased. They soon began using sophisticated grammatical and rhetorical terms to discuss their writing. More important, they began to apply this new knowledge to their writing. In other words, they became aware of what makes writing good, how it is judged, and how they can improve it. The majority of student comments confirmed a growing awareness of writing criteria and a rudimentary application of rhetorical skills. The assignment sequence was:

Day 1

- Students wrote a diagnostic essay, which the instructor rated according to the Test of Written English® (TWE®) guidelines, assigning a holistic score. However, scores were withheld until later.
- Homework: Write Journal #1: Write about the feelings you experienced when you had to write on the first day of class. How did you feel? Why do you think you felt that way? Is there anything you could have done to feel differently?

Day 2

- The teacher distributed a copy of the TWE rubric, which was explored as a whole class, defining jargon, and discussing rhetorical elements in the context of students' essays.
- Students examined a set of essays previously scored by TWE raters but with the scores removed. Students worked in groups to evaluate these essays according to the TWE scale, testing their newly acquired metalanguage about writing.
- Teachers showed students the scores assigned by TWE raters. A whole-class discussion followed in which students discussed the relationship between the essay scores they had assigned and those of the TWE raters.
- Teachers returned diagnostic essays written on day 1 with instructions to self-assess according to the TWE guidelines. Instructor scores were still unknown to the students.
- Following student self-assessment, teachers returned scores for the initial diagnostic essay.
- Homework: Students were to compare their self-assigned scores with the score assigned by their instructor. If the scores differed, they were to consult the TWE rubric, considering the reasons for any discrepancy.

Day 3

- Students wrote again on the same topic as the initial diagnostic essay to ascertain the efficacy of assessment criteria instruction.
- Homework: Journal # 2: Do you think your writing has changed from the essay you wrote on the first day of class to the second essay (on the same topic)? How did your writing change? Why do you think your writing changed? Did you learn something in class that you think helped your writing? What did you learn?

—Crusan & Cornett, 2002, pp. 22–23

When the researchers read their students' journals, they were surprised and happy to find that (at least on paper) it seemed that their students' understanding of writing and the ways in which it was assessed had deepened. Chief among the findings was the students' overwhelming preference for the fronting assessment criteria. Moreover, Crusan & Cornett (2002) found that following this protocol or one very much like it decreased the possibility of overt teacher bias. However, it is important to realize that bias exists in many forms and that it is not possible to totally eliminate it.

Peer Bias

Liu & Hansen (2002) define peer response as activities in which "students work together to provide feedback on one another's writing in both written and oral formats through active engagement with each other's progress over multiple drafts" (p. 1). Especially in peer response, student product may be affected in two ways. First, students often think they are unqualified (*their* bias) to comment on another student's writing because they are also L2 learners. Because they may judge themselves unqualified to make determinations about another L2 student's writing and wish to avoid being placed in the position of critic, they quite often simply tell their peer, "Oh, this is great!" When the writer submits the paper, he or she may find that the teacher's opinion of the work is vastly different from the feedback of his or her peers. Or the opposite response might occur where the peer points out every mechanical error to the exclusion of comments on the content of the writing. Whatever the case, such lack of critical peer review adversely affects students. The student is penalized if she submits a piece of writing that does not fulfill the criteria for the assignment, in part because the peer reviewer was not confident enough in her ability to comment on the work.

Despite the inherent problems in obtaining critical student feedback, Liu & Hansen (2002) contend that language learners can offer each other unique benefits in L2 writing classrooms. Students possess authority because they are readers and can comment on what they understand from a paper. Even if they are uncomfortable evaluating the mechanical aspects of the paper, certainly they can comment on its content, coherence, or logic. For example, if they are reading a story, can they follow it? Are there parts of the story that need to be better developed so the reader can get a better understanding of the intricacies of the plot? Are the events in the story clearly described? These are aspects of writing that students, with a little encouragement, can judge in each other's papers. The practice of peer review, a collaborative learning technique, will also lead to more critical readers and writers and will expose the students to different levels of writing abilities. See Liu & Hansen's 2002 volume for in-depth treatment of the many facets of and approaches to peer response.

To examine a second way in which student bias comes into play requires considering contrastive rhetoric (CR). Connor (2003) defined CR as a phenomenon that "examines differences and similarities in writing across cultures" (p. 218). Kaplan (1966) suggested that writers from different cultural backgrounds use different rhetorical strategies and that "language and writing are cultural phenomena" (Connor, 1996, p. 5). Kaplan (1966) maintained that the linguistic and rhetorical conventions of the first language hinder writing in the second language. For instance, suppose that the L2 students in a class are predominately from one country. Hypothetically, if the teacher pairs students with the same linguistic backgrounds and asks them to respond to each other's papers, the discourse markers, rhetorical modes, and stylistic aspects of their writing (superimposed on the L2) may not seem problematic because both students understand L1 cultural aspects and are looking at the L2 writing from the perspective of the rhetorical style of the first language. However, those same discourse markers, when interpreted in English, could pose problems if they do not follow the expected English rhetorical pattern. Conversely, different problems may surface when pairing two students with different L1s; their rhetorical expectations may be so different that neither can follow the other's writing. Fortunately, students can learn much from these exercises and can even help each other come to understand the rhetorical patterns at work in the L2 and how they might model them.

With respect to the efficacy of contrastive rhetoric, Connor (2003) expresses this caveat: "one needs to exercise care in attaching identifying labels to others' writing" (p. 224). Kaplan (2001) argues that although "CR has been criticized as a notion steeped in xenophobia and restrictive of the learner's freedom to experiment with deviant forms of discourse" (p. xv), CR can be better explained as "a notion designed to help learners manage the discourse structure of SASE (Standard American Schooled English)" (p. xv). From these standpoints, CR seems a useful addition to the L2 composition classroom.

Happily, peer response can be used effectively as a component of the composition classroom when considering the phenomena of contrastive rhetoric. Teachers can provide group assignments in which students are paired with students from different linguistic backgrounds. Again, because of differing rhetorical strategies, students are in a position to question meaning and form. Students in mixed groups reap several benefits:

- They will realize the need to address a mixed audience.
- They will come to understand that difference will always be one of the consistent traits of their audience.
- They will see the need to clearly create meaning for readers from a variety of learning styles, diverse cultural and language backgrounds, and rhetorical styles.

On occasion, it may be beneficial to group students of the same language background. For example, years ago, when teaching basic ESL writing, I would often allow students with the same language background to work together in peer response groups and even to use their first language if they felt they could clarify a concept. In one particular class, two homogenous groups (one Hispanic and one Vietnamese) met quite often; their papers reflected positively the effects of interaction in their L1.

Of course, there are limitations to this idea. First, because students are in an English class, they will, for the most part, be required to speak and write in English. Second, they need to be aware that their audience includes readers from other cultural backgrounds, that is, all the students in their class. And third, students matriculating at American universities should understand that professors in other departments will expect them to address written assignments from a Western rhetorical style, especially since many professors from different departments may not be familiar with the notion of contrastive rhetoric or the reasons for differences in writing style. Therefore, students may need to adopt a rhetorical style more typical to the United States, one that is perhaps quite different from that to which they have been accustomed.

Administrative Bias

Although administrative bias can be defined broadly, the focus here is on the penchant for some administrators to embrace standardized testing to the exclusion of all else. The focus is specifically on two groups of test consumers—administrators in universities and their notions and expectations of writing and writing assessment, and administrators of public schools who are currently bound by No Child Left Behind.

Often, university administrators believe that writing assessment, especially for placement purposes, should be done quickly, cheaply, and easily through the administration of a multiple choice assessment (Huot, 1994), which can be scored by Scantron® or a computer. Many schools, especially community colleges (Crusan, 2001; Lewiecki-Wilson, Sommers, & Tassoni, 2000) are marching in a direction not in alignment with current literature concerning writing assessment for placement, because they have adapted COMPASS-ACT®, a computerized assessment instrument in which examinees find and correct errors in essays on a computer screen. This reliance on assessment that is disconnected from actual writing conveys, more than anything else, an institution's definition of writing (Crusan, 2003) and the value it places on mechanical components of language rather than on language as a whole. Again, the adoption of such assessment methods demonstrates the importance administrators place on cost and convenience (Crusan, 2002a, 2003; Huot, 1994).

Direct assessment (often where students actually write and write in a specific amount of time like 30 minutes, and to a specific prompt; see Chapter 3) is more expensive and time intensive because raters need to be hired and trained. After students write, raters read the essays. This is a long process that psychometricians have labeled a "reliability nightmare" (Keith, 2003). Arguments (Cizek & Page, 2003) are that inter-rater reliability—what McNamara (2000) refers to as "quality control for raters" (p. 56)—remains low. So, for reasons of efficiency and reliability, many community colleges are again turning to indirect assessments ("objective" tests—generally multiple choice) as the preferred writing placement instrument, a giant step backward in the eye of most composition specialists (Lewiecki-Wilson, Sommers, & Tassoni, 2000).

In 1990, Hamp-Lyons celebrated the fact that the battle against indirect assessment of writing had been won, but some scholars (Crusan, 2002a; Huot, 1994) have found indirect assessment of writing in use at many institutions. In fact, both Haswell (personal communication, 2002) and Huot (personal communication, 2001) admitted that the percentage of institutions still using an indirect measure for at least placement purposes is much higher than originally believed. Huot's estimate is *75 percent.*

When clearly examined, this reliance on indirect assessment (at least for placement purposes) hardly classifies as surprising. Large, well-known, and respected testing companies, such as Educational Testing Services (ETS), McGraw-Hill, Houghton Mifflin, and Harcourt Educational Measurement, court administrators at every level of an educational institution that value efficiency, low cost, and quantification. They find the standardized offerings coupled with impressive sounding statistics provided by such companies attractive. Administrators seem to acquiesce because of the promise of reliable and valid writing assessment for a fraction of the time, money, and energy. However, they have been exposed to only one side of the assessment coin. When administrators succumb to the lure of cheap and easy, what happens to the voice of the teacher? Historically, teachers do not have the political capital or financial resources necessary to fight this power, and they lack the corporate backing that enables their positions to be heard by administrators or the public.

An Internet survey of websites of prominent universities in the United States (Crusan, 2002a), revealed that the universities investigated reported that they predominately used indirect testing for placement. Taking data on assessment for first-year composition placement of L1 and L2 writers from university websites, I found that "at least three of the largest and most prestigious universities currently use only a multiple choice instrument to place ESL students into composition courses" (p. 25). At the time of the investigation, one university was contemplating a switch to SAT II; although this is a step in the right direction for this particular institution (in the past it used a single 50-item multiple choice instrument to place both native and nonnative writers in first-year composition classes), a standardized test like SAT II does not adhere to the notion of locally designed instruments preferred by many writing assessment specialists (Hamp-Lyons, 1996; Haswell & Wyche-Smith, 1994; White, 1994). Unfortunately, once a testing method is in place and a bureaucracy is established, quite often there is considerable resistance to change as a result of inertia, job security, and a solidification of belief systems.

Anecdotally, one year at the TESOL Convention and Exhibition, an ETS employee asked to speak to me after my session, one in which I had been particularly critical of wholesale adoption of large-scale standardized assessment. Teachers like me can and often do bring assessment issues forward at their own conferences and in academic journals hoping that others will attend their presentations and read their articles; however, administrators rarely read the same academic literature as those fighting to maintain quality, authentic assessment in the classroom.

The problem is further compounded by political involvement in testing, especially sole reliance on high-stakes standardized testing, the dawning of No Child Left Behind, and the ways in which these ideas affect and enrich the testing industry. The trend is clear. In addition to becoming wealthier, testing companies are becoming politically powerful (Kohn & Shannon, 2002) through the public schools' over-reliance on standardized tests. Test developers are the principal benefactors in this quest for reliability and validity while schools, teachers, and students are being punished when they fail to meet standards that are often unrealistic, particularly for L2 students.

Principals and teachers are losing their jobs because schools and students have not been successful at meeting federally imposed criteria. (See *No Child Left Behind after Six Years: An Escalating Track Record of Failure,* 2008—www.fairtest.org/NCLB-After-Six-Years for a complete description of the backlash of mandated standardized testing.) However, administrators and faculty are not the only groups adversely affected: "Students' promotion to the next grade, their entrance into elite educational tracks, the careers of educators, and the reputations and budgets of schools increasingly hinge on standardized tests" (Brandon, 2002, p. 58). Further, the unintended impact of these tests on teachers in terms of lowered morale, lack of a sense of achievement, stress, anxiety, loss of independence, de-skilling, and resentment can, and is, driving qualified, caring educators from the classroom (Gallagher, 2007; McNeil, 2000).

All these developments and punitive measures spell problems for writing assessment in general and result in disastrous consequences for L2 writing assessment. A report on the effect of standardized testing ("How Standardized Testing Damages Education," 2007) claims that "students from low-income and minority backgrounds are more likely to be retained in grade, placed in a lower track, or put in special or remedial education programs even when it is not necessary. They are more likely to be given a watered-down or "dummied-down" curriculum, based heavily on rote drill and test practice. This only ensures they will fall further and further behind their peers" (p. 1). Therefore, it is vital that our profession speaks loudly and clearly, that teachers publicize the downside of standardized writing assessment in the classroom, to boards of education, volunteer boards for adult education, and university trustees. Teachers need to be the voice of reason and should offer information (Hillocks, 2002; Kohn & Shannon, 2002; Shohamy, 2001).

Political Bias

It is critical to consider political bias and raise awareness of the ways in which our thinking, and thus our assessments, might be influenced. How, one might ask, does political bias affect L2 writing assessment? The answer really is quite simple. The population in general of the United States is conservative at best in its thinking about education and assessment (Crusan, 2009; Gallagher, 2007; Kohn, 2000; Kohn & Shannon, 2002; Shannon, 2007). Easy fixes are all too often used out of context as the sole or primary remedy for important educational issues. However, "as norm-referenced, standardized assessments rarely help teachers make instructional decisions (other than to teach to the test), it is critical that teachers conduct appropriate formal and informal assessments that are tied to their instructional goals" (Samway & McKeon, 1999, p. 62). It follows then that teachers need to know how to create assessment tools.

Political bias can be defined as that bias that occurs at all governmental and educational levels to justify using specific tests to validate politically motivated goals. These goals may include:

- justifying the need for additional funds, the need for additional programs, or the need to cut spending.
- documenting improvement (in scores) of a population of students or discriminating against culturally and linguistically diverse or educationally disadvantaged students.
- improving public perception of student progress or evoking a public response that a crisis exists.

- rewarding or punishing specific teachers, administrators, or school systems; consolidating a political or administrative power base or removing an entrenched administrative hierarchy.
- helping politicians make names for themselves.

Additional components of political bias include:

- **misuse bias**—using a test for an unintended purpose or for an untested application.
- **spin bias**—interpreting aggregate test scores in a way most favorable to promote a political agenda.
- **test developer bias**—reporting in or advocating the use of specific standardized tests based on basic (simple statistical) measures of reliability; often neglecting higher order biases since they are too difficult to measure or evaluate.
- **statistical bias**—relying only on those parameters that are relatively easy to measure as an indication of the universe of implications, inherent biases, and reliability of the tests.
- **self-definitional bias**—defining a student's ability as being able to score at a specific level on a standardized test, leading to results that are self-referential.
- **higher order biases**—any form of bias including political bias and its components as well as consequential validity and validity generalization.

Understanding the biases presented in this chapter is vitally important as it encourages us to critically examine our own biases and preferences when we assess our students' writing abilities. Too often, L2 writing teachers attempt to assess their students without a clear understanding of their own biases or the implications of their assessment decisions. The writing assessment field has evolved substantially over the past few decades, yet it seems to me that few outside the assessment community have implemented the pragmatic aspects of the assessment of writing. Certainly in the academic world, writing assessment is critically important; however, teachers often feel themselves outside the realm of assessment, blocked by the language of testing professionals, stymied by quantification, and confused by rhetoric from the standardized testing community. Yet, they are forced to teach for standardized tests of questionable value to either the teacher or to the ultimate consumer, the student.

Suggestions for Teachers

1. Interview your principal, superintendent, department chair, dean, director of writing programs, or director of testing in an effort to understand who controls assessment at your institution.
2. At parent-teacher conferences, ask parents their opinions on high-stakes testing and what advantages or disadvantages they see, especially as it affects their children.
3. Ask your students to help create their own assessments including the rubrics and criteria by which they will be graded. Ask them how they believe they can be fairly assessed.
4. Prior to each writing assignment, critically evaluate the prompt for possible bias. Then after grading the assignment, determine if any cultural group performed better or worse than expected.

   As a class, discuss the ways in which students have felt/feel that they have been victims of some sort of bias or prejudice. Discuss ways in which they can help educate others to be more accepting of diversity.
5. Ask your students to try to construct a bias-free prompt; have the class critique the prompts.
6. Create a community of writing assessment experts within your school who can design and implement local assessments.

Suggestions for Further Reading

For more views regarding the politics of assessment in general and the politics of writing assessment in particular, see Shohamy's *The Power of Tests* (2001); Kohn & Shannon's *Education, Inc: Turning Learning into Business* (2002); Hillocks' *The Testing Trap: How State Writing Assessments Control Learning* (2002); Gallagher's *Reclaiming Assessment: A Better Alternative to the Accountability Agenda* (2007); and Shannon's *Reading Against Democracy: The Broken Promises of Reading Instruction* (2007).

Chapter 5

Large-Scale Writing Assessment and Its Influences on L2 Writing

Any time an indicator takes on too much value, it is corrupted and so are the people around it. If test scores take on too much value, educators, like all other human beings, are likely to manipulate the indicators.
—David Berliner

Testing is often at the forefront of the news. A review of U.S. testing history shows that standardized tests have evolved rapidly over the past century and have become a potent force in education (*Washington Post,* 2006). States were expected to spend between $1.9 and $5.3 ***billion*** dollars by 2008 to implement NCLB-mandated tests (Miner, 2004/2005). In 2007, Virginia estimated that state implementation costs totaled approximately $20 million per year; Connecticut estimated the cost of complying with NCLB at $17 million (Lips & Feinberg, 2007).

As tests have become more prevalent, so too has the business of test preparation. This phenomenon is not restricted to the United States, however, but is international in scope. China's New Oriental Education and Technology Group, Inc., offers exam prep at 35 schools and more than 130 learning centers, mostly in eastern China (http://english.neworiental.org). Best known as a "cram" school, the size of New Oriental (2008 net income estimates range from $183.93 million to $197.32 million) is testimony of the scope, impact, and importance of standardized testing in China and further evidence that testing (including test preparation) is indeed big business. Clearly, testing and test preparation are burgeoning industries.

This chapter explores an overview and description of large-scale writing tests for L2 writers, advantages and disadvantages of standardized tests of writing, political and business aspects of large-scale assessment, the effect of NCLB legislation on the L2 writer, and strategies for classroom teachers to make large-scale writing assessment work for their students.

An Overview of Large-Scale Writing Tests: Product and Purpose

This section describes tests generally used for large-scale writing assessment of L2 writers living both within the United States and internationally. Many of these instruments assess the skills of reading, speaking, and listening along with writing. Five tests that include a separate writing section and have consequences for both U.S. and international L2 writers at levels from high school to graduate school will be discussed: TOEFL®, TOEIC, SAT, ACT, and GRE. The advantages and disadvantages of these types of tests follows.

TOEFL®

The TOEFL®'s stated purpose is to assess the English proficiency in reading, writing, speaking, and listening of non-native speakers of English. ETS claims that international L2 test takers will be eligible for admission into "virtually any institution in the world—including the top colleges and universities in the U.S., Canada, U.K., Australia, and New Zealand" (www.ets.org/). Currently, ETS offers two versions of the TOEFL®—the paper-based test (PBT) and the Internet-based test (iBT). According to the ETS website (www.ets.org/portal/site/ets/), the PBT has three sections, and one of the sections, Structure and Written Expression, "measures the ability to recognize language that is appropriate for standard written English" (ETS, 2008b). The test consists of 40 multiple choice questions to be answered in 25 minutes. Also required of everyone taking the PBT is a 30-minute writing test, the TWE® (Test of Written English®). Examinees are asked to respond to prompts such as

- What are some important qualities of a good supervisor (boss)? Use specific details and examples to explain why these qualities are important.
- Some people think that the family is the most important influence on young adults. Other people think that friends are the most important influence on young adults. Which view do you agree with? Use examples to support your position.

Two readers rate each essay using a 0–6 point rubric. Readers either score at home or at ETS scoring centers using ETS' Online Scoring Network (OSN) (Weigle, 2002). OSN is a secure Internet system that provides a platform for the display of test-taker responses, support materials for raters, and tools for monitoring the accuracy of raters (ETS, 2008c). The score assigned to an essay is derived by averaging the two independent ratings or, in the case of a discrepancy of more than one point, by the adjudication of the score by a reading manager. For an example of a rubric, see Weigle, 2002, or the ETS website.

The writing portion of the iBT is comprised of two tasks, integrated writing and independent writing. The integrated writing task requires examinees to combine two or more skills (reading, writing, listening) to respond to a question; this integrated skills approach asks examinees to write based on what they have read and heard. After examinees read a short passage, they listen to a lecture. Note-taking is allowed. Next, examinees are asked to use the information from the reading and the lecture to write (in 20 minutes) an essay in which they present the points in the lecture and how they relate to the reading. The second task asks examinees to support an opinion on a topic. The topics are similar to the TWE® on the PBT:

The writer has 30 minutes to complete the essay. Each task has a separate rubric, specifically created for the task. Although these are five-point rubrics, the scores are converted to a 30-point scale. ETS provides these guidelines for writing proficiency:

- Limited (1–16)
- Fair (17–23)
- Good (24–30)

According to the iBT website (www.ets.org/portal/site/ets), ETS-certified experts score responses online using OSN. This iBT rubric is very much like the PBT rubric, although it's based on five points instead of six.

TOEIC®

The TOEIC® purports to measure the ability of L2 speakers to use English in everyday work activities. According to the TOEIC website (www.ets.org), English is the global standard for business, and thus, nonnative speakers of English must be able to communicate effectively in English in order to function in a global economy.

ETS claims that TOEIC can be used by universities, colleges, and schools as well as business, industry, and government for a variety of purposes: to prove the effectiveness of an English language program, as an instrument to place students into courses, and as an assessment for exit from a program. In late 2005, speaking and writing components were added to the TOEIC. ETS further claims that students can use the test to track their progress as they learn.

The writing portion of the test was introduced in 2006. Students are given 60 minutes to complete the three sections that are delivered through the same online system as the iBT writing test. The test includes integrated tasks that simulate actions common in business such as reading an email and responding.

Example of TOEIC® Writing Test Tasks		
QUESTION	TASK	EVALUATION CRITERIA
1–5	Write a sentence based on a picture	• Grammar • Relevance of the sentences to the pictures
6–7	Respond to a written request	• Quality and variety of your sentences • Vocabulary
8	Write an opinion essay	• Whether your opinion is supported with reasons and/or examples • Grammar • Vocabulary • Organization

Scores range from 0–200, and scoring is through OSN using ETS-trained and ETS-monitored raters. Potential examinees can purchase practice tests and receive scores from ETS to help them know where they need to improve.

The SAT

It might seem strange to discuss the SAT in a book about assessing L2 writing and writers because the SAT is generally considered a test for native speakers of English, specifically high school students in the U.S. seeking admission into American universities. In the United States, Generation 1.5 students are defined as U.S.-educated students who

- might consider themselves bilingual.
- come from a family that speaks a language other than English at home.
- possess social skills at a seemingly native level.
- lack native level skills in academic writing.
- may not be able to write in the L1 of their home. (Harklau, Losey, & Siegal, 1999)

These students will be required to take the SAT to gain admission into U.S. colleges and universities. In addition, the SAT is administered in 243 countries, territories, and foreign states including the Holy See (Vatican City State).

According to its website (www.collegeboard.com) the SAT is taken by more than two million students every year and is the instrument most accepted for admission purposes by virtually all American colleges and universities. The College Board claims that the SAT measures classroom knowledge in reading, writing, math, and a student's ability to apply that knowledge outside the classroom. Further claims relate to the SAT's capacity to help colleges acquaint themselves with potential students' reasoning, problem-solving, and communication abilities. The College Board continues to maintain its long-standing position that the SAT (along with high school grades) is the best predictor of college success.

The writing portion of the SAT consists of two sections—a multiple choice section (35 minutes) and an essay (25 minutes). The multiple choice section features questions that test students' ability to improve sentences and paragraphs and identify errors related to verb tense, syntax, word usage, and subject-verb agreement. The short essay, written by hand, asks examinees to develop a point of a view on an issue (in 25 minutes) using reasoning and evidence—based on experiences, readings, or observations—to support ideas. A sample writing prompt is:

Think carefully about the issue presented in the following excerpt and the assignment below.

Many persons believe that to move up the ladder of success and achievement, they must forget the past, repress it, and relinquish it. But others have just the opposite view. They see old memories as a chance to reckon with the past and integrate past and present.

- Adapted from Sara Lawrence-Lightfoot,
I've Known Rivers: Lives of Loss and Liberation

Assignment: Do memories hinder or help people in their effort to learn from the past and succeed in the present? Plan and write an essay in which you develop your point of view on this issue. Support your position with reasoning and examples taken from your reading, studies, experience, or observations.

www.collegeboard.com/student/practice/writing-sat-essay

College Board–trained high school and college teachers score the essay. Each essay is reviewed by two different readers, who give the essay a score from a low of 1 to a high of 6 based on the overall quality of the essay and demonstration of writing competence. Neither rater knows the other's score, nor do the raters know writers' identities.

The ACT

The ACT also claims to be "America's most widely accepted college entrance exam" (www.act.org/aap/index.html), maintaining that more universities both require and prefer the ACT. Consequently, L2 writers, particularly Generation 1.5 writers, might be required to take the test. The ACT assesses high school students' general educational development and their ability to complete college-level work. Interestingly, on its website, the ACT compares what it measures with what the SAT claims to measure, stating that the ACT "measures achievement related to high school curricula, while the SAT measures general verbal and quantitative reasoning" (www.act.org/aap/concordance/index.html).

The ACT is a multiple choice instrument that measures skills in English, math, social studies, and science. Examinees are given 45 minutes to take the 75-question, multiple choice English test. The questions are designed to test vocabulary, grammar, punctuation, and other subskills of writing. An optional writing test measures a student's ability to plan and write a short essay in 30 minutes. The test provides two different perspectives of an issue and asks examinees to support one or develop their own. An example ACT writing prompt is:

> Educators debate extending high school to five years because of increasing demands on students from employers and colleges to participate in extracurricular activities and community service in addition to having high grades. Some educators support extending high school to five years because they think students need more time to achieve all that is expected of them. Other educators do not support

extending high school to five years because they think students would lose interest in school and attendance would drop in the fifth year. In your opinion, should high school be extended to five years?

In your essay, take a position on this question. You may write about either one of the two points of view given, or you may present a different point of view on this question. Use specific reasons and examples to support your position.

Two trained readers evaluate each student's essay, each giving the essay a rating from a low of 1 to a high of 6. Those two scores are combined to arrive at a writing subscore ranging from 2 to 12. A discrepancy of more than one point between the two raters results in a third reading. In addition to numerical scores, writers are provided with "positive and constructive feedback on their essays in the form of reader comments" (www.act.org/aap/writing/sample/rubric.html).

GRE®

The GRE®, taken by students seeking admission into graduate programs, is offered worldwide and accepted by graduate programs internationally. The test "measures verbal reasoning, quantitative reasoning, critical thinking, and analytical writing skills that are not related to any specific field of study" (www.ets.org/portal/site/ets/menuitem). Currently, ETS offers two versions of the test—a paper-based test and a computer-based test. The computer-based general test is made up of 30 multiple choice questions (30-minute time limit), 28 multiple choice quantitative questions (45-minute time limit), and two analytical writing tasks, one issue task (45 minutes) and one argument task (30 minutes). The issue task offers two prompts; the examinee chooses one. The examinee has no choice of prompt for the argument task. Although the multiple choice section of the paper-based test varies from the computer-based version, the writing section is in the same format on both tests.

The GRE **issue** task looks like this:

TOPIC 1:

"Both the development of technological tools and the uses to which humanity has put them have created modern civilizations in which loneliness is ever increasing."

TOPIC 2:

"Our declining environment may bring the people of the world together as no politician, philosopher, or war ever could. Environmental problems are global in scope and respect no nation's boundaries. Therefore, people are faced with the choice of unity and cooperation on the one hand or disunity and a common tragedy on the other."

(www.ets.org/portal/site/ets/menuitem)

Examinees are free to accept, reject, or qualify the claim made in their selected topic; however, the ideas presented must be clearly related to the topic. Examinees are instructed to support views with reasons and examples from their reading, experience, observations, or academic studies.

The GRE **argument** task is as follows:

The following appeared in a memo from the director of a large group of hospitals.

"In a laboratory study of liquid antibacterial hand soaps, a concentrated solution of Nadasept killed 40 percent more bacteria than the liquid hand soaps currently used in our hospitals. During a subsequent test of Nadasept at our hospital in Saluda, that hospital reported significantly fewer cases of patient infection than did any of the other hospitals in our group. Therefore, to prevent serious patient infections, we should supply Nadasept at all hand washing stations throughout our hospital system."

(www.ets.org/portal/site/ets/menuitem)

Examinees are instructed to discuss how well reasoned they find the argument. They are asked to develop ideas fully, organize them coherently, and leave time to revise.

Prior to 2008, two ETS-trained raters scored the written portions of both the paper-based and computer-based GRE using a 1–6 holistic scale. The reported score, an average of the two, is reported in half point increments (e.g., 4.5). However, in October 2008, ETS implemented e-rater scoring technology for the computer-based GRE Analytical Writing section. Developed by ETS, e-rater is a computerized natural language-processing program. After human scoring, e-rater reviews the essay score, monitoring the human reader. If the e-rater evaluation and the human score agree, the human score is used as the final score. In case of discrepancy, a second human score is obtained, and the final score is the average of the two human scores. See Chapter 7 for a more thorough explanation of the machine scoring of essays.

Advantages and Disadvantages of Standardized Tests of Writing

Many teachers view standardized testing as problematic. Testing is big business. In the United States, the business of K-12 testing is largely dominated by three test publishers—Harcourt Educational Measurement, CTB McGraw-Hill, and Riverside Publishing (a Houghton Mifflin company)—and one scoring firm—NCS Pearson, the leading scorer of standardized tests. Harcourt, CTB McGraw-Hill, and Riverside Publishing write and produce 96 percent of the exams administered at the state level (Educational Marketer, October 2001). Educational Testing Services is perhaps the largest test developer for the higher education market, especially for the international market (TOEFL®, TOEIC, and others) although its status as a nonprofit shields it from disclosing its financial standing.

Customarily, many of the advantages of standardized testing relate to issues of validity, reliability, and objectivity—matters that are possibly of more direct concern to test developers than to teachers, but it would be imprudent to discount these features. First, standardization ensures a certain level of objectivity. Of course, one can argue that no test is objective, as someone is determining the "right" answer, but standardization does offer a more reproducible and arguably more accurate evaluation of the subset of skills that the test measures. Further, grading is standardized, perhaps lessening scorer bias and possibly ensuring comparable test scores regardless of scorer.

Some standardized test companies claim that their tests predict how well students will perform in colleges and universities. For instance, the Medical College Admission Test (MCAT) tests aptitude necessary for medical school. While a good MCAT score does not guarantee success in medical school, Julian (2005) claims, "Grades (in medical school) were best predicted by a combination of MCAT scores and undergraduate GPAs (uGPAs), with MCAT scores providing a substantial increment over uGPAs" (p. 910). However, it is important to notice that this increase in predictability is due to a combination of factors and not based solely on one test score. What is more, such tests do not consider students' maturity, social skills, dedication, empathy, or creativity.

Another advantage of standardized testing is that the results can be generalized and repeated, which determines a test's validity and reliability. An additional benefit stems from data resulting from aggregate (the combination of all test-takers') scores, which, some claim, offers a more precise assessment of a particular group's skills and knowledge. An individual test-taker's score alone cannot indicate how well the test measures the body of knowledge for which it has been designed; however, because the pool of test-takers is so large, the aggregate scores do supply useful information simply because, statistically, as sample size increases, error decreases. Finally, although critics of standardized tests claim bias (see Chapter 4 for discussions of various biases), the tests do offer a uniform and reproducible means of evaluating applicants against others (www.standardizedtests101.com). And for what it's worth, this is the real purpose of tests like TOEFL® and SAT®: to measure applicants' performance against other applicants and ease the admission process (for the admissions committee).

While these advantages are important, and since high-stakes testing is so pervasive, it is critical to examine the disadvantages of standardized testing as well. One of the most problematic is the use of one single score, on any test, as a global indicator of the collected knowledge or intelligence of a person. A single score on any test may not accurately evaluate the test-taker's abilities, skills, and knowledge; yet, in many instances, particularly under the current implementation of No Child Left Behind, students, teachers, and certain school administrators are held accountable based on a single score on one test instead of multiple measures (GPA, extracurricular school activities such as sports and clubs, community service, multiple intelligences [Gardner, 2006]), which may more accurately indicate students' strengths and weaknesses. Haswell (1998), addressing placement procedures for second language writers, created a "list of commandments" (p. 162) for better ESL placement. One of his commandments concerns the need for multiple samples of a student's writing in order to make well-informed decisions about the writing classes into which L2 writers should be placed.

Another issue looms large—the <u>use</u> of test scores—particularly a *single* test score. Teachers lose jobs, districts lose funding, and students lose confidence when they do not perform well on standardized tests. One of the problems with single score use centers around results of studies (Orlich, 2007; Orlich & Gifford, 2007) that continually link parental income with students' test scores, confounding the results and invalidating their use as sole indicator of just about anything. Orlich (2007) found extremely high correlations between parental income and scores on the ACT (r =.99) and SAT (r =.97), finding that as a child's parental income goes up, so do the ACT and SAT scores; as parental incomes decreases, so do the scores. One test score—of any skill for any student—clearly is not the best indicator of students' abilities.

The College Board added an essay to the SAT in 2003. The reaction to this was mixed. One of the college composition community's concerns was the possibility that the combined score does not measure what it purports to measure, in this case the ability to produce a well-developed essay. For one thing, according to the College Board website, the SAT multiple choice writing section counts for approximately 70 percent and the essay counts for approximately 30 percent of the total raw score (www.collegeboard.com/student). Evidently then, on this test, the subskills of writing (vocabulary, grammar, mechanics) that can be measured through a multiple choice instrument are weighted heavier and are apparently deemed as more important than actual writing. Further, the "SAT I Writing Assessment elicits a snapshot of students' performance in writing" (Hamp-Lyons, 2005, p. 154) rather than using multiple examples of student writing produced over time and addressing different audiences and purposes. These two realities—the indirect assessment of writing coupled with a snapshot approach—quite clearly demonstrate potential drawbacks of the College Board's definition of good writing.

Another issue with the SAT essay test and similar standardized tests of writing concerns the narrowing of the writing curriculum in schools coupled with the teaching of formulaic writing. Curriculums become narrowed when schools reduce the amount of time spent on subjects that are not tested (e.g., history, music) and focus only on those subjects that are formally tested, such as math and literacy. The kind of writing that is generally required on standardized tests (even though the companies who create the tests argue to the contrary) is a very narrow kind of writing—in effect the five-paragraph essay: "While the impromptu essay will say to the schools that writing matters, it will reinforce the teaching of formulaic and unreflective writing, even as it will discourage the innovative approaches to placement now going on in many universities" (Hamp-Lyons, 2005, p. 154). In general, the term *formulaic* translates into the four- or five-paragraph essay. Certainly though, we should not demonize the four- or five-paragraph essay; it has a transitional place in the teaching of writing and can be very helpful to L2 writers as they learn the necessary and expected format in academic institutions. However, for large-scale, high-stakes testing, L2 writers need to be taught the formula that includes an introductory paragraph with two to three main points listed at the end of the paragraph, two to three paragraphs developing each of the main points, and a concluding paragraph summarizing the essay. They also need to know that this formula is a scaffold or framework on which to build. Championing the five-paragraph essay as authentic writing misleads students about the kinds of writing that is expected of them as they enter colleges and universities.

Another disadvantage to this kind of writing is that it most often is timed. The timed essay, once applauded as a welcome departure from the multiple choice measures used in the past to evaluate students' writing ability, is now considered far from authentic (White, 1995; Hamp-Lyons, 2005), especially when used as a final exam. Authentic assessment is a form of assessment in which students are asked to perform real-world tasks that demonstrate meaningful application of essential knowledge and skills (Brown, 2004). Timed essays do not allow for the reflective thinking or multiple revisions that encapsulate authentic text production. Mueller (2008) (http://jonathan.mueller.faculty.noctrl.edu) compares traditional assessment with authentic assessment by setting up the following continuum in which traditional assessments fall more toward the left end of each continuum and authentic/alternative assessments fall more toward the right end.

Traditional	**Authentic**
Selecting a Response	Performing a Task
Contrived	Real-life
Recall/Recognition	Construction/Application
Teacher-structured	Student-structured
Indirect Evidence	Direct Evidence

When viewed in this light, the timed, or impromptu, essay seems artificial and inauthentic. However, in response to attacks on the use of the impromptu essay test, White (1995) reviewed the strengths of this type of essay compared with the indirect methods of assessment for writing placement. While the impromptu essay test is viewed less favorably than in years past due to the development of portfolio assessment, White believes that the timed essay represents a compromise, calling it more valid than multiple choice alternatives and more efficient in terms of time and cost than portfolio assessment. However, the recent inclusion of a required essay on the College Board's SAT has caused a flurry of discussion about the reliability of a timed essay as a measure of writing ability, especially in regard to its effect on second language writers. The College Board acknowledges this issue on its FAQ page, with this answer to the question of whether the new SAT test is fair to all students:

> We do not expect any minority group, including ESL students, to see any significant differences in their relative performances on the new SAT as compared with the previous test. Research from a spring 2003 field test involving more than 45,000 students, as well as research on the previous SAT, shows that ESL students and minority groups perform on writing as well as or better than on critical reading measures. (www.collegeboard.com)

White's support of the timed essay as a placement alternative still leaves questions regarding its usefulness as an in-class measurement of writing ability. Why might we continue its use? If there is a pedagogical purpose for its use, if the essay allows students to see what it might be like to write under pressure for a test situation in another course (e.g., history, psychology, sociology), then writing the essay is valid. If one of the goals is to prepare students to cope with essay exams across the curriculum, teachers can ask students to write a timed essay at any time during the term to provide them with that experience.

The Politics and Business of Assessment

The link between assessment and politics is pervasive but often not recognized by teachers or students. Many assessments at the institutional level represent a series of gates through which the writer must pass (or hoops through which the writer must jump). These include state-mandated writing assessments, writing assessment on large-scale admissions tests, assessment for placement, and exit assessments that determine students' ability to write well enough to graduate from college. These are all high-stakes assessments and carry with them political motivation, particularly when the mandating institution selects the actual tests to be used.

Tremmel (2003) reminds us that "we cannot disconnect the political from the educational, and, though we may not all realize it, we cannot profess an apolitical stance in our teaching" (p. 1). Teaching is a political act, often performed in resistance to outside pressures that mandate (but often do not pay for) standardized testing and the lockstep curricula born out of that mandated testing. Metcalf (2002) argues that standardized testing, especially that mandated in the NCLB, "emphasizes minimal competence along a narrow range of skills, with an eye to satisfying the lower end of the labor market" (p. 2). He further argues that global competition forces the business community to focus on the relationship between money spent on schools and test scores. Although this input/output argument can be a shallow way to look at the education of future generations, it is a common business model.

Of course, teachers understand that schools shape the development of future generations of citizens and workers and are an important source of jobs and investment in many communities. Most teachers are also painfully aware that political institutions and philosophies within and outside schools manipulate the content, form, and function of instruction (Shannon, 2001) and influence matters such as reform and innovation, privatization and school choice, race and ethnicity, poverty and inequality, professionalization and bureaucratization, and testing and accountability.

Freire (1970/1993) linked education to social change, asking that teachers problematize student learning by compelling learners to engage with the complexity of a notion or a task, demanding that they see the world in many shades of gray rather than in only black and white. He called for teachers to discover a more reciprocal relationship (teachers learning from students, students learning from teachers, students learning from students) in the classroom, rather than a dichotomous one in which the teacher is the source of all knowledge and responsible for stuffing that knowledge into students' heads. Freire (1985) also believed that teachers should engage in a dialectical process of reexamining the development of their own learning experiences and the problems they encountered. In this way, as with the idea of problematizing student learning, the educator might discover better methods. However, problematizing, building reciprocal relationships, and reflecting on one's teaching take time, intense thought, effort, and discussion. Teachers are hesitant to engage in such higher-order practices when the all too powerful bureaucrats around them are clamoring for higher test scores, test scores that represent minimal competence in a narrow range.

The actions and decisions of our elected officials impact our classrooms at every level. When something is termed *political,* we say that it is *carried out for reasons that serve a desired outcome rather than for reasons that are, for example, morally justified.* We can examine writing assessment in light of this definition. Why do we assess writing? Teachers of writing need to see how students write so that they can help them become better writers; that is, teachers examine students' writing with an eye to improvement through feedback and encouragement, using written comments and writing conferences. However, the assessment of writing becomes an even more political issue when those doing the assessment cannot agree about what constitutes good writing let alone *how* to assess writing. Lines are drawn, and sides are taken. This seems to happen more at the institutional level. Often administrators view writing assessment as motivated by political rather than educational concerns, as well as concerns about time, money, and ease of administration.

The Effect of NCLB Legislation on the L2 Writer

Interestingly, while implementation of NCLB in schools with a large population of limited English proficient (LEP) students has resulted in some problems for ELLs' education, "the net effect of the law has been positive because it has (1) increased attention paid to ELL students; (2) increased the alignment of curriculum, instruction, professional development, and testing; and (3) raised the bar for ELL student achievement" (de Cohen & Clewell, 2007). Resulting accommodations may include tests designed specifically for the population, the use of translators, dictation of answers, extra test-taking time, repetition of directions, and the use of bilingual dictionaries.

So why all the fuss? One wearisome notion in large-scale assessment centers on *norm referencing*. Norm-referenced tests set goals for students based on the average performance of a population of students; in other words, they compare a student's score against the scores of others who have already taken the test and then represent that with a percentile rank. When a student is said to be in the 75th percentile, for example, that means she performed better than 75 percent of those who took the test; however, a relative score really says nothing about how this student actually writes. Further, because most norm-referenced tests are reflective of the content of nationally used textbooks, students may not have been taught the specific material being tested if their school district uses texts and sources other than those used by testing companies.

There are additional issues to consider. Under NCLB, schools face consequences such as state takeover or privatization if their students do not perform well on standardized tests. These high-stakes consequences have a direct impact on practice. First, they cause subjects to be dropped from the curriculum if they are not on the test (Kohn, 2000; Shannon, 2007; Valdez-Pierce, 2003). In other words, if a subject is not covered in any way on the test, it will quickly vanish from being taught in the classroom.

Social justice is another concern: "Many educators locate current testing practices within the history of marginalization and discrimination against immigrant students in U.S. public schools" (Menken, 2005, p. 236). In some cases, ESL classes have been eliminated so that students could prepare for tests in content areas (Monroe, 2006). Compounding things, fewer resources are available to ELLs since these students are "disproportionately low-income and more likely to attend lower-resourced schools" (Neill, 2005, p. 1).

According to Nichols & Berliner (2007), high-stakes testing has become a barrier for students whose first language is not English. Many of these students do not understand the test, resulting in arbitrary answer choice. ELLs may feel humiliated and worthless. So it is not surprising that ELLs typically perform worse than other students on standardized tests, resulting in serious short- and long-term consequences for them (Menken, 2005). For example, often when ELL students produce less than adequate results, they are sent to learning disability classes, keeping them from interacting with high-performing peers (Monroe, 2006). Other unintended consequences include increased dropout rates, retention in lower grades to ensure preparation for the test, high expulsion and suspension of ELLs before testing days, omission of nontested subjects (music, art, science) from the curriculum, teaching to the test for extended periods of time, fact memorization, teacher attrition, cheating by teachers and administrators, and even excluding ELLs' scores from reports (Kohn, 2000; Menken, 2005; Monroe, 2006; Nichols & Berliner, 2007).

However, as this book goes to press, the Obama administration is considering changes to the accountability systems and prescriptive interventions of No Child Left Behind.

Strategies for Making Large-Scale Writing Assessment Work

At the present time, teachers have little recourse than to make sure that ELLs are prepared to take the standardized tests that NCLB demands. What are some of the ways that teachers can help students to succeed? First, be educated about tests. Obtain access to disclosed copies of the test. Then deconstruct the test to find what kinds of vocabulary and terms students need. Deconstruct the test design—make lists of key words often used. Look at how the test is written. What does a standard writing prompt look like? What does the prompt call for? Usually, the prompts ask students to take a stand about an issue and defend it or to compare and contrast two ideas or questions.

Next, create test savvy students. Share with your students the information you uncovered in your test deconstruction. Show them how you determined what the test requires. Then give students a list of prompts and work through them to determine what the prompt is asking for and the best way to approach it. Spend a little time teaching students how to take the test, how to read the directions, how to color the bubble-shaped ovals on the answer sheet. Whatever skills students need, provide them. Learning how to prepare for tests is a form of cultural capital (Delpit, 2006) that, many ELLs, because of socioeconomic status, may not possess, unlike their upper–middle class peers. We must also provide reading instruction—some students might not be good readers. Read to students and enlist parents to do the same, if possible (there may be language issues involved).

Teachers can also create writing savvy students. Instruct them in the kinds of writing that a standardized test requires (usually the four- or five-paragraph essay). Teach them how to write for the test, carefully pointing out that the kind of writing required on the test is rarely the kind of writing done in real life. Then practice. Use sample writing prompts and assign them for homework. In the process-oriented writing classroom, teachers can create a writing workshop where authentic writing and authentic writing assessment take place. Make time for in-class peer and teacher feedback on homework assignments. Ask students to create rubrics and peer feedback sheets based on their understanding of what the test demands. In this way, the requirements of the test will be cemented in their minds. Many other activities can help develop the writing skills of students:

- Write letters to the editor of the local paper about an issue of concern to the class.
- Write letters of complaint about a product that was below student expectations.

- Write email messages requesting information for a field trip.
- Write movie or video game reviews, compile them, and publish them.

Make testing a game to be won. First, literally play games to increase the vocabulary of L2 writers. Use word searches, crossword puzzles, hangman, matching, and word unscrambling. Establish writing contests with prizes for the best story, the fewest grammar and punctuation errors, or the most words used from recent vocabulary lessons. Incorporate writing into homework activities. Even if it goes against your basic philosophy of teaching, practice taking tests. Teach students that they can crack the code of the test. Teach them about distractor items, and practice finding these distractors in sample questions. After they are found, place students in groups and ask them to write rationales for why they think their selections are the distractors. Then ask them to write their own multiple choice questions. Always ask why, and teach students to ask why, to analyze, to critique.

For students preparing for the SAT, the ACT, or the TOEFL®, the instruction can be very much the same. Copies of TOEFL® prompts are readily available on the Internet. With these, teachers and students can deconstruct prompts, look for key words, and, as a group, determine what those key words refer to and what they might look like in an essay. What does a well-developed essay look like? Teachers can also provide sheets with tips for doing well on the writing test, such as:

- Read the statement carefully, and make sure you understand it.
- Make the parts of your essay easily identifiable.
- Write carefully or type in a font that is easy to read.
- Make sure you answer the entire question.
- Know the rules of English punctuation.
- Use sentences that are brief and to the point.
- Use examples and details to support your ideas.
- Use a variety of sentence structures.

Finally, and perhaps most important, share the scoring rubric with students and teach them what the items on the rubric mean. What are unity, coherence, and progression? What does an organized essay look like—what words can be used to help the essay be organized? When teachers help students decode the test and the rubric, much of the mystery and scariness can be removed, helping students see that they can excel on the test.

Suggestions for Teachers

1. Be informed. Visit the website of the department of education in your state. Many provide sample tests, answer keys, and scoring rubrics.
2. Attend school board meetings in your community to find out the district's policies on English language learners.
3. Conduct a 45-minute to 1-hour interview (face-to-face or on the telephone) with an established school board member, employee of a testing company, teacher, superintendent, principal, department chair, university professor, university admissions officer, university or school district testing coordinator, dean, state legislator, or governor. Your goals for this interview are to draw on your interviewee's experiences with testing and determine his or her philosophy regarding assessment, particularly assessment of English language learners.

Suggestions for Further Reading

For a comprehensive discussion on standardized tests of writing including purpose, content, scoring, construct, and usefulness, see Weigle (2002), Chapter 7.

Chapter 6

Innovative Technology in the L2 Writing Classroom

Any sufficiently advanced technology is indistinguishable from magic.
—Arthur C. Clarke

This chapter examines several technological innovations and their effects on writing assessment in the L2 writing classroom: synchronous and asynchronous communication tools, online paper mills, online writing centers, and the outsourcing of assessment and other functions of the writing classroom through online instruments. Teachers of L2 writing need to be proactive to retain control of what they teach in their writing classrooms, how they teach writing, their relationship to specific writing technologies, and, in particular, how and with what technologies they assess the writing their students produce.

Technology in the Classroom

Teachers are becoming increasingly dependent on technology in the classroom, and because of this technology, teaching now is different from how it was even five years ago. Not long ago, teachers distributed paper syllabi on the first day of class, dispersed hard copies of handouts detailing assignments and grading criteria, used the chalk-board and overhead transparencies to communicate important concepts, and relied on TV and VCR for media viewing. Although most of these technologies are still used, many teachers find themselves in wired classrooms using smart desks equipped with computers, monitors, and various presentation options including elaborate projector systems for viewing Microsoft® PowerPoint™ presentations, websites, and movies. The Internet, for better or worse, is at a teacher's fingertips. Suites of applications (e.g., *Course Studio*), which create and manage course homepages, links, articles, and files to disseminate class materials, are popular. Students come to class armed with laptops and USB Flash Drives and access papers and presentations through their email accounts.

At my institution, all composition courses, both for L1 and L2 writers, are taught in computer classrooms where students compose on computers, submit written work electronically to their peers and instructors, and receive teacher and peer feedback electronically. Instructors conduct classes on networked learning environments such as WebCT, Blackboard, Moodle, Desire2Learn, and Elluminate®. Some classes only meet online. Others are hybrid versions that feature both face-to-face and online meetings. This array of impressive technology and its innovative use in classrooms leaves teachers with the question of how much of this technology is a boon to writing pedagogy and to the writing abilities of students. Teachers need to consider the impact that each component of technology has on teaching, on teaching writing, and, particularly in this chapter, on writing assessment.

Using Synchronous and Asynchronous Technology for Assessing Writing

Before deciding to use any technology, teachers should ask themselves what purpose a specific technology will serve in the classroom (Bloch, 2008). It's important to understand how *computer-mediated discourse* [CMD] (Bloch, 2008) or *computer-mediated communication* [CMC] (Blake, 2008) can best help teachers improve and assess student writing. Currently, there are two forms of CMD/CMC—asynchronous and synchronous. *Asynchronous* computer-mediated discourse is commonly facilitated by media such as email and discussion boards and supports communication among learners and teachers, even when participants cannot be online at the same time. Asynchronous platforms make it possible for learners to log on to an environment at any time and download documents or send messages to teachers or peers.

At the most basic level, email provides a tool for writing assessment/feedback as it allows teachers to comment within an email or to attach documents to which they have provided feedback.

Using Synchronous and Asynchronous Technology for Assessing Writing

Before deciding to use any technology, teachers should ask themselves what purpose a specific technology will serve in the classroom (Bloch, 2008). Prior to making a decision, teachers need to understand how *computer-mediated discourse* [CMD] (Bloch, 2008) or *computer-mediated communication* [CMC] (Blake, 2008) can best help teachers to improve and to assess student writing. Currently, there are two forms of CMD/CMC—asynchronous and synchronous. *Asynchronous* computer-mediated discourse is commonly facilitated by media such as email and discussion boards and supports communication among learners and with teachers, even when participants cannot be online at the same time. Asynchronous platforms make it possible for learners to log on to an environment at any time and download documents or send messages to teachers or peers.

At the most basic level, email provides a tool for writing assessment/feedback because it allows teachers to comment within an email or to attach documents to which they have provided feedback. However, the recent Educational Records Privacy Act (ERPA) places some restrictions on what can be sent to students. For example, feedback including a grade—

"right now this paper will earn a B, but you can improve your grade with the following revisions"—would be a violation of ERPA. Feedback without a grade—"you can make this paper stronger with the following revisions"—would probably be acceptable.

Discussion boards are excellent tools for writing assessment because the writing students submit is seen by both their peers and their teacher—automatically enlarging and making their audience more authentic. As a result, students may think more carefully about their contributions to these platforms, leading them to be better assessors of their own writing, one of the goals of most writing courses. Bloch (2008) adds, "Since asynchronous discourse allows the participant as much time as needed to think and compose a message, it may help the students with weaker language skills to respond in ways that are just as complex as those of students with stronger language skills" (p. 131). As an added bonus, discussion boards, long considered one of the fundamental tools of asynchronous distance learning (Blake, 2008), allow weaker writers the opportunity to observe the ways stronger writers use and manipulate language. Further, because discussion threads can be saved, examples of teacher and strong student writing are available for reference of both ideas and language use.

Second-generation asynchronous Internet tools (Blake, 2008) provide many benefits for self-assessment, peer-assessment, and teacher feedback and assessment. Two such tools are blogs and wikis. With blogs (a blend of the words for *web* and *log*), writers use multiple forms of media to communicate with people from around the world. Blogs are easily editable webpages with posts or entries organized in reverse chronological order (Zawilinski, 2009). Lenhart & Madden (2005) report that 12 million adolescents aged 12–17 maintain blogs in the United States. Students routinely use blogs to communicate outside of school on topics of all kinds. When used in the classroom, students benefit from the broad audience this form of communication provides. Increasingly, teachers have discovered the many benefits of blogs: connecting in-school and out-of-school literacies, integrating writing in a way that supports reading, and developing higher-order thinking (Zawilinski, 2009).

Craddock (2009) describes the writing and writing assessment that happens, as an example, on a Harry Potter fansite/ blog—MuggleNet.com—where writers post fan fiction, a collaborative genre to which possibly thousands of readers and writers contribute. Almost immediately after a submission has posted, readers read and respond. If the response is positive, it is generally posted on the blog comments section; however, negative comments are generally made through the more private email format. This truly tests a writer's ability to draft and revise. Craddock's point—that most of the course outcomes of composition courses—using writing as a generative tool, drafting and revising with response from readers, critical reading and analysis, identifying, assessing, and presenting best work—are being accomplished for real purpose and real audiences. Particularly important is the self-assessment piece. However, when used in the classroom, blogs must be intentionally designed and valued in the curriculum. They cannot function merely as an add-on or students will not be as motivated to participate in them. Moreover, when students are allowed to personalize some of the postings (e.g., their poetry, comments on what they are reading outside the classroom), they are more invested; hence, the blog becomes more valued and a better instructional tool (Zawilinski, 2009).

Wikis—Hawaiian for *quick* (Blake, 2008)—are examples of collaborative writing. Wikis are free online writing spaces. No specialized knowledge of HTML or HTML tools is needed to create or use a wiki. Since they are a group product, any member of the group can modify content. Because of the group interaction on a wiki, any modification affects all participants. Collaborators can observe how others interact with text, how changes in the text change meaning, and the importance of precision, concision, and clarity. Wikis can be used to debate assigned readings, share resources, and encourage collaborative revision. When used as a collaborative writing tool, students witness the power of peer suggested revision and the shared planning of writing conventions used on the wiki.

Computer-mediated synchronous communication is simply communication that happens at the same time (real time) such as exchanges in a chat room, on Skype, or on course management systems like Elluminate®. Synchronous communication might be difficult for L2 writers as it is quick and they may have difficulty following along (Bloch, 2008). However, when used as a means for audio student conferencing about their writing—what Bloch (2008) refers to as "electronic tutorial" (p. 138)—many of the benefits of face-to-face meetings [e.g., simplifications, elaborations, confirmation and comprehension checks, clarification requests, or recasts (Blake, 2008)] are available. Using the voice tool available on Elluminate®, a real-time virtual classroom environment designed for distance education, learners and teachers might avoid frustration by asking and answering questions in real time. Further, with a platform such as Elluminate®, users can share their desktops or any document on their desktops, allowing conference participants the opportunity to view the student's paper and scroll through the paper. In this way, students can ask questions about their papers and receive immediate feedback from their teacher, a peer, or a tutor. Other benefits of synchronous CMD include lowering of students' affective filters because "no one is looking over their shoulders as is the case in face-to-face meetings" (Blake, 2008, p. 77). Additionally, with the chat feature, students have more time for linguistic processing to prepare their own contributions (Blake, 2008). Additionally, because Elluminate® has both text and voice features, students can respond in the way that they are most comfortable.

Even with these advantages, technology might not be a good thing in all instances. Bloch (2008) reminds us that the introduction of technology can radically alter the second language writing classroom. He questions ways in which technology affects literacy and cautions that technology is not <u>the</u> answer to writing problems. On the other hand, technology is not flawed in and of itself: "A middle ground has emerged that assumes that technology is neither transparent nor deterministic, neither inherently good nor bad. This position is often referred to as 'technorealism'" (Bloch, 2008, p. 8). Today's teachers must carefully negotiate this middle ground, and they must be educated in the ways of teaching composition online and about the impact that online teaching has on the assessment of writing.

The Impact of Technology on L2 Writing Assessment

Along with the influence of technology on writing and the teaching of writing, the use of technology in the writing classroom is having a major (and sometimes positive) effect on writing assessment. Linguists know that language is never static, and a heavy reliance on technology and the accompanying language changes could foster even more definitions of good writing.

Weigle (2002) argues that writing is becoming more speech-like, citing the use of email and discussion boards for this evolutionary change in direction. Might these new forums in turn impact writing assessment and even our definitions of good writing? She argues, too, that networked classrooms uncover the more social aspects of writing; such use of technology eases communication and allows for easy sharing of work. In terms of writing with computers in the classroom, Weigle challenges teachers who assess writing to think not only of the linguistic aspects of writing but to consider the metacognitive ones as well. What skills must a writer have to navigate these different purposes and audiences? Are these valuable skills for the future? Will the notion of good writing change? She claims that "the most successful papers may not be the ones with the most well-formed sentences and felicitous word choices, but the ones whose authors have reflected on their peers' comments and have used this feedback to hone their arguments and ideas to meet the expectations of their audience" (p. 233). No one would disagree that the ability to convey well-thought-out ideas and well-formed arguments through writing is a valuable skill of our students.

While some teachers worry that cellular telephone text messaging and instant message (IM) shorthand, for example, might adversely affect the syntax, spelling, and grammaticality of their students' writing, this technology, at the very least, has students using written language more. On one level, technology has been responsible for an increase in both the quantity and quality of students' writing. Lewis & Fabos (2005) report that participants in their study examining the functions of IM "manipulated the tone, voice, word choice, and subject matter of their messages to fit their communication needs, negotiating multiple narratives in the process" (p. 470). And in a study examining the impact of web-based software on elementary students' personal narrative, Englert, Manalo, & Zhao (2004) found that students wrote more, incorporated more genre-specific characteristics, and exhibited conventional writing skills when they wrote a paragraph in a supported, web-based environment. A supported paragraph environment provides genre-related scaffolds to students, reminding them to generate topic sentences and add supporting details, among other things, certainly a positive outcome from the use of technology.

ODSP

Another positive use of technology concerns assessment for writing placement of incoming freshmen at institutions of higher education. Using Royer & Giles' (1998) groundbreaking work in directed self-placement as a framework and encouraged by administrators, I created an online directed self-placement instrument [ODSP] (Crusan, 2006). Students log on to a secure site, and from that site, L1 students enter demographic information and respond to a series of statements, both cognitive and affective, about their writing habits. A sample of the 20 statements are:

- I like using computers to draft and revise writing.
- I turn in assignments on time, and no one has to remind me to get the work done.
- Generally I don't read when I don't have to.
- In high school, I wrote several essays per year.

One of the most positive aspects of ODSP is its inclusion of L2 writers, previously excluded from self-placement. At those earlier face-to-face sessions, directed self-placement (DSP) counselors (all writing instructors from the English department) greeted students and explained what would happen during the session. At this point, DSP counselors asked non-native speakers to identify themselves as such, and then they were required to write an essay, instead of being allowed to engage in the self-placement process. Some at the institution believed that L2 writers were not equipped to adequately judge their writing proficiency in English. Meanwhile, L1 students watched a PowerPoint presentation, which informed them about the composition classes offered and the kinds of writing skills students needed in order to succeed in each class (Crusan, 2006). Eventually Wright State's ODSP included L2 writers; when the department was under new management.

L2 writers responded to a slightly different list of statements, such as:

- I can revise my papers written in English without the help of a native speaker of English.
- I regularly translate from my native language when writing in English.
- I worry about sharing my writing with native speakers of English.
- I am unsure of the rules of writing in English, and I struggle with grammar and punctuation.
- I am nervous about writing in English.
- I have written an essay/paper/book review/memo in English in response to something I have read.

Although this placement method (Crusan, 2006) has come under fire because it does not include real writing, White (2008) has recently called directed self-placement "a radical solution to the persistent problems of over testing, negative labeling, and student initial discomfort with required coursework" (p. 139). Many writing assessment scholars (Crusan, 2002a; Huot, 2002; White, 1990, 1996b) believe that the best way to judge writing is through writing. Due to mandates from the Ohio Board of Regents and the governor of Ohio elected in 2006, writing programs are now required to use the score on the ACT English test or the SAT writing test as a placement indicator. So ODSP has been retired at Wright State, and we are once again using an essay. Now second language students (regardless of the presence or absence of test scores) must complete the writing placement test, but the test is now a response to a reading accessed online, a more authentic task. Also, once students log on to the test site, they have 72 hours to complete and submit their writing, which may possibly better reflect real writing. Be that as it may, it is important for the teachers who teach second language writers to be involved in how and where they are placed. If that is not possible, then teachers should certify student placement during the first class by administering a diagnostic essay that can serve dual purposes: assuring that students are correctly placed and providing the teacher with information about the writing ability of the students in the class.

The Dark Side of the Internet: Paper Mills

Technology complicates classroom-based assessment. Of major concern is a pervasive form of plagiarism using Internet paper mills. Typing the single keyword *essays* into Google's search engine retrieved literally millions of results. Thousands of essay topics, written by custom researchers working in teams, are available with a 24-hour turnaround time. Sites offer essays that claim to be nonplagiarized, cheap, high-quality, and written for specific assignments. Some offer free bibliography pages in any citation style and free unlimited amendments. In reality, these essays are far from cheap, costing nearly $100 for a five-page essay with reference page(s).

With so many sites offering these essays for sale, it would seem that many students are far more concerned about their grade on a product than with the discovery of knowledge or with learning new writing skills. Of course, the availability of papers-for-sale is not new; paper mills have long been in existence. It is just much easier to obtain topic-specific papers now thanks to the Internet.

Nevertheless, teachers can combat student use of paper mills by informing their students that they know about the sites. Also, by using a pedagogy that encourages multiple revision, peer review, and teacher-student conferences, teachers can be more confident that the writing they see is indeed the writing of their students.

Combating Internet Plagiarism

What messages do writing-for-sale websites send to students about writing? How is writing valued? Is writing something to have experienced, a process through which something is learned, or is writing about the product? The paper mill websites, of course, clearly align themselves with product, and if writing teachers are entirely honest, we cannot deny that we expect a product from our students. Of course, if teachers manage a process-based classroom in which students revise multiple drafts of the same essay before a final grade is attached, they can hope that their message of thoughtful process gets through to their students, at least in composition classes. Still, how long will it be until these sites offer portfolio services complete with incremental improvements in content, style, and mechanical and grammatical surface errors in response to the feedback L2 writers receive from classroom teachers and peers?

If teachers and students are operating in a portfolio-based, multiple draft composition classroom environment where teachers know the kind and quality of writing their students produce, what market exists for Internet sites such as EssayFinder.com and its counterparts? I would guess that students make far more extensive use of Internet paper mills to obtain papers for classes like sociology, psychology, history, religion, philosophy, and similarly required general education courses, classes in which instruction is centered on content rather than on learning to compose and in which required multiple drafting is rare, classes for which courses in composition are preparing students.

The online paper mill might also be a still larger issue for students whose first language is not English. Certainly, students who are struggling with not only the topic but also the language might easily succumb to the lure of sites offering easy solutions to troublesome (in their view) and time-consuming writing assignments. Of course, teachers might more easily detect L2 writers' use of online paper mills because downloaded essays do not contain L2 language issues.

If L2 writers use Internet paper mill sites, what is the long-term cost to them? What if they have not acquired or developed basic writing skills—have they squandered their best opportunity to improve their writing skills in a supportive environment? Possibly. Whatever the case, it seems that, at least from their sheer number, these ubiquitous paper mill sites are a popular, profitable, and often utilized staple of the Internet. However, teachers armed with information about the easy accessibility of writing-for-sale can alert students to the fact that their teachers are aware of at least some of what's out there in cyberspace. Additionally, teachers who manage a process-based classroom and use alternative assessment methods (e.g., portfolios) can reduce the probability of plagiarism.

Outsourcing of Grading

Another major innovation—the use of technology to replace some or all of the feedback and assessment duties traditionally performed by writing teachers—worries many faculty. Of course, this is not to say that all teachers distrust technology (although some do); however, educators need to strike a balance with its use, and neither banning it from the classroom nor using it exclusively. Instead, critically examine when and how to use technology in the L2 writing classroom. At least for now, some applications of technologies may not be in the best interest of our students, particularly L2 writers. Two topics particularly worthy of close scrutiny are (1) the outsourcing of feedback and grading using online tools, and (2) the machine scoring of essays (see Chapter 7).

It is not uncommon to read about companies who outsource jobs to other companies and other countries in an effort to increase productivity and lower costs. Many universities outsource bookstores, food services, and, in some cases, housing. Even the most overworked composition teachers who read and respond to hundreds of papers each term (the market targeted by outsourcing-of-grading companies) might be surprised by the proliferation of programs and people offering to take the burden of assessing writing from them. (See Chapter 7 for a discussion of assessment as burden or drudgery.) On the surface, the concept seems benign enough, especially since teachers in U.S. junior and senior high schools may see more than 180 students each week and international EFL teachers may have 60 or 70 students in one class. However, a closer look beneath the rhetoric reveals a far different and possibly more risky reality. Let's examine a few of the programs currently on the market with an eye to how these online grading companies influence the definitions of writing and the value of assessment as a central component of any teacher's job.

EduMetry

EduMetry (www.richfeedback.com/index.html) is a "one-stop assessment service." The rationale for its existence, at least in the United States, is the accountability movement. Overall, the company claims that, because of the clamor for accountability, what is needed is a clear measurement system that explicitly demonstrates learning outcomes to outsiders and supplants the implicit system understood by insiders (*standardization*).

In response to this demand for clarity, EduMetry provides design and implementation of large-scale assessment projects on a university-, campus-, or college-wide basis. It claims that faculty have no time to be involved in large-scale assessment projects because of teaching, service, research, mentoring, and professional development demands. EduMetry further argues that its services cost less than what it takes to maintain an in-house complement of assessment experts. These justifications may be particularly attractive to administrators struggling with budget constraints. However, those whose employment might be affected may not view EduMetry's rationale for outsourcing with dispassion.

EduMetry also offers grading services for faculty; rationalizing that educators "have better things to do than read and respond to their students' work." These services are called OutScore™ and Assess+™. Both methods score what EduMetry calls "student learning-artifacts" (www.richfeedback.com/assessment.html) and generate student learning outcomes data. OutScore™ uses rubrics to score a representative sample of learning artifacts. These scores are used to generate data for use at the college-, program-, and cohort-level of aggregation. Assess+™ claims to provide students with "detailed and actionable" feedback on learning artifacts and provides instructors with summative reports in real time (within 2 to 5 days of receiving electronic submissions).

SMARTHINKING

SMARTHINKING is another outsourcing venue. Providers of the world's largest online writing lab, the developers of SMARTHINKING bill themselves as an online tutorial service that "helps students succeed" (www.smarthinking.com). The company capitalizes on something that teachers know is true—instructors, particularly writing instructors, are stretched too thin. But the company approaches the problem from a different angle—that is, it seems to think that relieving the instructor of notions such as conferencing with students and assessing students' work will be helpful. In reality, these are the very things on which teachers should be focusing, because this is how teachers discover what students know and where they need help. Further, the more urgent problems of class size and teaching load are the larger issues that must be dealt with in any composition program, whether L1 or L2. In fact, administrators might even compound the problem of class size and teaching load after adoption of an online program such as SMARTHINKING or *WriteSpace*. They might reason that since teachers' heavy burden of providing feedback to their students and grading their work has been lifted, they can now manage an increased class size and possibly teach more sections. Indeed, one of the selling points on the SMARTHINKING website is "giving your instructors more time to work with MORE students" (www.smarthinking.com/). Could such programs soon become the tipping point in the de-skilling of teachers and the depersonalization and commercialization of education? (*De-skilling* refers to teachers "who become simple deliverers of content and skill processes rather than those who intricately synthesize content, skills, and concepts to create sophisticated curriculum designed to meet the needs of their particular students" [Rice, n.d., p. 1].) The websites for outsourcing services (SMARTHINKING, etc.) are clearly directed at administrators. Writing program administrators (WPAs) should not only be informed about these programs but should also be positioned to answer questions that university administrators may ask about these programs and to present arguments against the widespread, uninformed adoption of such programs. Teachers certainly need to be prepared with convincing language and well-informed answers when asked to consider adoption of any programs that take control away from writing programs and teachers and place that control into the hands of business.

One of the daunting issues surrounding these writing/tutorial programs is the direction of future developments of this technology and its tendency to expand into related markets. Some of these programs are now touted as tutorials, but language such as "Let us do the grading" seems to be sounding a death knell for teacher grading of student work.

Again, two of the major grievances of composition teachers are course load and class size. What is to keep an administrator from enlarging class size, course load, or both after realizing that an outside contractor can grade student work? Can the savings be so substantial? Possibly. When institutions factor only direct costs such as benefits and salary, online tutorials might seem to be the economic salvation for which administrators have been praying. SMARTHINKING provides just that kind of cost-effectiveness evidence: "We are able to address our students' writing needs across the curriculum without creating the management infrastructure, quality control and staffing for an on-campus writing lab . . . SMARTHINKING's qualified, trained, and monitored tutors allow us to provide our students with the high quality writing instruction that we demand at a savings of over $20,000 per year" (Dr. Willard Lewis, President—Isothermal Community College, www.smarthinking.com/). The primary issue of inadequacy seems to have been, however, overlooked. How might some faceless tutor know our students better than we do? How can meaningful feedback be provided? If assessment drives instruction, and I contend that it certainly does, teachers need to be primary sources of feedback and assessment in order to make pedagogical decisions about their next steps in the classroom.

Other Products

Writing-related products are being developed every day, including some that claim to provide feedback for writing students. Some are intended for very specific help and show proper formatting for articles, books, and reports. Others, like **StyleWriter** (the plain English editor), claim to be "ten times more powerful" than any grammar checker with the ability to "edit and polish writing into clear and concise English" (www.writersupercenter.com/stylewriter/). Still others claim to do everything: teach, tutor, give feedback, and grade.

In the era of NCLB legislation and the move to standardize education in the United States, study after study has reported that the single variable most often correlated with high achievement—particularly high test scores—is socioeconomic class (Emery & Ohanian, 2004; Graves, 2002; Hillocks, 2002; Ohanian, 1999). It stands to reason that families of a higher socioeconomic class populate schools with a stronger economic base; more money leads to more access opportunities, whether that access is to better buildings, better materials, or better technology.

A significant problem with corporate tutoring programs rests with the idea that they are not developed for the individual and incredibly diverse populations at each institution but instead are large, decontextualized, mass-marketed, composition-as-a-business tools. Scholars (Crusan, 2006; Ferris, 2002; Hamp-Lyons, 2003; Huot, 2002; White, 1995, 1996b, 2007) have long argued that those who know their students best—the teachers—should teach them, give them feedback, and assess their work. The same can be said for the outside help students seek for their writing. While some grammatical issues (e.g., the difference between *there, their,* and *they're;* article use; and general punctuation questions) might be easily handled through a decontextualized site, a locally based writing center would be much more familiar with the assignments students are given, the instructors who teach the courses, and the teachers' expectations of both their students and the writing center. For example, at my institution, teachers fill out surveys about how they would like the writing center to handle specific writing issues. For instance, do they wish students to receive grammar help? Do they allow tutors to suggest changes in content? Can an outsourced site provide this kind of contextualized help with student writing?

In the future, as web-based help evolves to a more useful level of sophistication, we still must question the covert costs to institutions, teachers, and students with respect to the social aspects of writing and the de-skilling of teachers. Further, we must consider the impact that web-based help will have on the ability of creative students and special needs students to be nurtured and encouraged on an individual basis.

In an attempt to keep writing assessment and writing assistance local, many institutions have established online tutoring help at their institutions; however, few, if any, incorporate live online chats and real-time interaction with students. For the moment, online tutoring consists mainly of helpful links that address things such as essays' introductions and conclusions, methods of citation, and help with the mechanics of writing. The lure of the online chat and synchronous online tutoring through live Internet chat is powerful to students, even if they have to pay for it. Thankfully, some universities have begun to offer such services.

While technology has substantially developed in sophistication in recent years and has attempted to entrench itself as a useful classroom tool, it has led to numerous problems. Many questions remain: Who is in charge of the classroom? Is it the writing teacher, who along with her students makes the decisions about what is important to learn and what good writing embodies? Or is the teacher merely a figurehead and record-keeper dependent on outsourced electronic feedback and tutoring? Further, if we allow this technology to enter our classrooms, how do we determine its impact on our students? And once introduced, is the decision reversible? Many questions still need to be answered.

Suggestions for Teachers

1. Investigate some of the writing-for-sale Internet sites. How might you combat the use of these in your classroom? Are there possible uses (other than actually buying papers) for these sites?
2. Examine one of the following websites and take the tours offered or sign up for a free trial.
   - www.TutorVista.com
   - www.editorsforstudents.com/tutors.html
   - www.writeshop.com/onlinetutoring.htm
   - www.etutoring.org/
3. Once you have examined some online tutoring websites, think about how they might be useful in the L2 writing classroom. List ways in which you think they can help students be better writers. List disadvantages to their use as well.

4. Now think about how a teacher might incorporate some applications into his classroom without relinquishing control of the classroom.
5. Investigate computer availability, software availability, computer usage, and professional development for teachers regarding the use of technology in their teaching. Choose a school near you. Contact a teacher of ELLs and, if she is available, conduct an interview. Present your findings in class. Some questions you might consider asking the teacher:
   - How many computers are in your classroom?
   - How often are students able to use computers?
   - For what purposes do students use computers?
   - What kind of Internet connection is available?
   - How much training have you received in using computer technology?
   - How comfortable are you with Internet research?
   - What are the keyboarding skills of your students?
   - What other issues about using computers in the classroom concern you?

Chapter 7

Looking Beyond: What Can We Expect of Writing Assessment in the Future? The Machine Scoring of Essays

Technology makes it possible for people to gain control over everything, except over technology.
—John Tudor

Several notions loom large for the future of writing assessment. One of them is the supposed benefit of the machine scoring of essays. The day may come when computers will be able to do what humans do today. However, analysis of text is an incredibly complex undertaking (Warschauer & Ware, 2006). In an interview conducted by Pontin (2006), Danny Hillis says, "We look to our minds and watch our patterns of thought, reasoning, planning, and making analogies and we think, 'That's thinking.' Actually, it's just the tip of a very deep iceberg. When early artificial intelligence (AI) researchers began, they assumed that hard problems were things like playing chess and passing calculus exams. Those applications turned out to be relatively straightforward. But the types of thinking that seemed effortless, like recognizing a face or noticing what is important in a story, turned out to be very, very hard" (p. 1). In fact, Hillis believes that creating a machine capable of truly thinking like a human being, with all of the complexities of the human brain, would require solving dozens of interrelated difficult problems, a task that no one yet knows how to accomplish.

Machine Scoring of Essays Defined

In the most basic terms, the machine scoring of essays is defined by the industry as computer technology that evaluates and scores writing (Shermis & Burstein, 2003). The machine scoring of essays has several aliases: automated essay scoring (AES), automated writing evaluation (AWE), automated essay evaluation (AEE) (Burstein, Chodorow, & Leacock, 2004), and automated essay grading (AEG) (Grimes, 2005). McAllister & White (2006) contend that the term generally used by the industry—*automated essay scoring*—is a misnomer. They claim that "virtually none of the work in computer-assisted writing assessment is automatic to the point of being autonomous yet, but rather requires numerous human-computer interactions; thus, computers are assisting in the partially automated writing assessment process" (p. 246). However, no matter what we call the machine scoring of essays, we still need to focus on its use and control its use in our classrooms and institutions.

Despite the limited progress in the entire field of artificial intelligence, companies touting products purported to automatically score essays and provide feedback to writers aggressively advertise that their products *are* able to deal with the complex nature of the mind and the writing process. As for machines thinking like humans, Moravec (1998) likens computer technology to a gradual flooding of the landscape. He claims:

> As the rising flood reaches more populated heights, machines will begin to do well in areas a greater number can appreciate. The visceral sense of a thinking presence in machinery will become increasingly widespread. When the highest peaks are covered, there will be machines that can interact as intelligently as any human on any subject. The presence of minds in machines will then become self-evident. (p. 12)

It is clear that there are at least two diverse perspectives to the machine scoring issue. These sides are often confrontational, much as they are in writing assessment in general. White (1990) first noted this confrontational aspect of the writing community and the measurement community when he attended a meeting of the Assessment Forum of the American Association for Higher Education (AAHE). Despite having been at the forefront of writing assessment for some time, White was stunned that the sessions he attended featured presenters whose assumptions about writing assessment were absolutely foreign to him. He remarked that he viewed these different ways of thinking about writing assessment as "a conflict between discourse communities, between ways not only of reading the world but also of writing the world, of seeing and making sense of what we see" (p. 189). Later, White (1996a) worried that continuation of this division would reinforce the notion that the assessment activities that went on in the classroom had no connection with the assessment activity that happens outside our classrooms. This division is no clearer than in the discussion of the machine scoring of essays. Not surprisingly, an analysis of the benefits of machines scoring essays differs depending on which perspective one holds; at least presently, the line has been clearly drawn between the academic, testing, and measurement communities.

As expected, the academic perspective as articulated by Broad (2006) reminds us consistently of "the necessity of human relationships and interactions in the evaluation of rhetorical abilities" (p. 233). Breland (1996), acknowledges the politics of science versus the humanities and also acknowledges that a dialogue regarding the use of technology in writing assessment must include not only scientists, engineers, and computer programmers, but also writers, teachers of writing, and other humanists with a less technological bent" (p. 250).

Electronic grading *might* be a great benefit to students who want to write more than teachers can read; programs such as WriteToLearn™ (Pearson Education) or Criterion℠ Online Writing Evaluation Services (Educational Testing Service [ETS]) advertise their services using this type of phrasing. Admitting that while it is unlikely that computerized grading will ever replace the careful eye of a teacher, these companies maintain that online writing programs can be a great addition to the writing classroom as they offer students the opportunity to write more and receive a greater amount of rapid feedback. They argue that teachers are unable, because of the immense time commitment, to read enough to provide students with adequate feedback.

Shermis & Burstein of ETS (2003) invite writing teachers to become involved in the enterprise. They write:

> The fact that automated essay scoring is not yet perfect is both a blessing and a boon. It is a blessing insofar as the invitation is still open for all members of the writing community to become involved to help shape future developments in this area. It is also a boon because it is open to criticism about the current lack of features relevant to writing. Will the technology identify the next great writer? Probably not. But does it have the promise of addressing most of the writing in the classrooms? Certainly. (p. xv)

If Shermis and Burstein are to be taken at their word, the L2 writing community should ask how to become involved and inquire into the venues for input.

Not surprisingly, many writing teachers' first reaction to the notion of a computer responding to (let alone *scoring*) their students' writing is one of dismay; at least I see that emotion written on my colleagues' faces when I mention this phenomenon to them. Their rejoinder may seem quite understandable if they fear the possibility that computers might one day replace teachers. (Even the more staunch supporters of the machine scoring of essays do not explicitly make this claim.) However, as researchers and teachers, we certainly recognize the need to thoroughly examine implications, advantages, and disadvantages prior to making a decision about using (or not) any of the many platforms available to score the writing our students produce. White (1990) calls on us to try and understand the language of our colleagues even if it conflicts with our own because we are "limited by what we know and the language that lets us know it" (p. 199). It is imperative that teachers not rely solely on gut response. For teachers to be current and informed about this topic, all perspectives need to be studied and understood; we must educate ourselves about the machine scoring of essays and, particularly, its implications and suitability for L2 writers. Only after a thorough and fair examination can we make informed choices about this rapidly changing technology. We should keep in mind the Japanese proverb: *Bad and good are intertwined like rope.*

This chapter examines various views regarding the use of machines to score student writing, situates machine scoring in the context of composition theory and writing assessment theory, and explores both the consequences and possible benefits of using these systems in L2 writing classrooms. After reading this chapter, teachers should be ready to resist well meaning but perhaps uninformed administrative changes in writing programs at their institutions—in this instance, the possibility of an unexamined *wholesale* acceptance of automated writing programs and machine scoring.

All commercial programs are dependent on an assortment of proprietary algorithms. An algorithm is a mathematical procedure for solving a problem, a predetermined list of well-defined instructions for accomplishing a task. The accuracy and versatility of even the most sophisticated algorithm is dependent on (1) the underlying assumptions, (2) the proficiency of the human raters used (see page 163), (3) the quality of the associated database, and (4) the weighting of the various component features being analyzed. Who selects the essays that will serve as the baseline calibration standards for the rating program? What is their definition of good writing? Are these algorithms flexible and sophisticated enough for diverse writers and their texts? Although supporters claim objectivity as a reason to use these programs, the programs are still very subjective. Further, the very proprietary nature of the programs hinders direct comparison of the strengths and weaknesses of their components.

Origins of the Machine Scoring of Essays

The history of the machine scoring of essays is a long and extremely complex one. McAllister & White (2006) provide a detailed report concerning the rise of "computer-assisted writing assessment, which is a subdiscipline of natural language processing, which in turn is a subdiscipline of artificial intelligence" (p. 16). For nearly 30 years, text-checkers—computerized spell-checkers, grammar-checkers, and style-checkers—have been employed to analyze students' text. Haswell (2005) reports that, despite inaccuracies in text-checkers, relatively little has been done to improve their accuracy for the past 25 years by the major software development companies. (See Haswell [2005] for an in-depth history, chronology, and bibliography of text-checkers.)

In 1966 Ellis Page developed the first documented essay scoring machine (Page, 2003), the Project Essay Grader (PEG), which used computerized methodology to grade student writing. Page's first program counted things like prepositions and conjunctions, which he called *proxes* (Elliot, 2005, p. 221), and in 1968, he "designed an experiment in which grades established by computer tabulation of approximately thirty proxes correlated well with grades assigned by four human judges" (p. 221). Page foretold the future, seeing computer essay scoring as creating an impact on the assessment world. However, computer stability in the 1960s was a major problem, so interest died until the 1980s when relatively stable microcomputers were developed (Warschauer & Ware, 2006). Page's enthusiasm never waned, and he continued his work until his death in 2005. Throughout the years, interest in the machine scoring of essays has grown to the point that most established test development firms in the United States now have at least one platform for the machine scoring of essays.

To date, the literature on the machine scoring of essays consists of a few books (Ericsson & Haswell, 2006; Shermis & Burstein, 2003) and numerous articles and conference presentations. Most published articles appear in journals seldom read by composition teachers, such as *The Journal of Technology, Learning, and Assessment; Journal of Information Technology Education; IEEE Intelligent Systems* (which bills itself as the #1 magazine in artificial intelligence); and *Journal of the American Society for Information Science.* Conference presentations have been largely from the industry side of the issue (although that continues to change as more L2 writing researchers begin to study machine scoring from a more pedagogical perspective). These presentations fill the programs of conferences not well attended by writing teachers, such as the International Conference on Research and Development in Information Retrieval, the International Association for Educational Assessment, the Workshop on Using Toolsets and Architectures to Build Natural Language Processing (NLP) Systems, and the Workshop on Computer-Mediated Language Assessment and Evaluation of Natural Language Processing. Conference programs that focus on composition, such as the CCCC, TESOL, the WPA Conference, the Symposium on Second Language Writing, and others, list very few presentations on automated scoring systems, and of the few sessions that are offered, most are given by industry affiliates. As a result of the limited availability of such sessions, few composition teachers attend these sessions, and few have the expertise to challenge industry positions or assumptions. With the barrage of industry-sponsored information being presented at national conferences—complete with charts, technical jargon, and sophisticated statistical analysis, it is little wonder that administrators with one eye on the budget and the other on standardized test scores uncritically accept industry viewpoints and have begun incorporating the technology.

The body of work of Jill Burstein, Mark Shermis, and others associated with the automated essay scoring industry is quite impressive. These industry voices are repeatedly and eloquently heard extolling the virtues of the machine scoring of essays, leaving administrators with a rather one-sided perspective regarding the pros and cons of machine scoring of essays, especially the suitability of such programs for second language writers.

The opposite perspective from the classroom has received less attention although that is changing rapidly. Work by Ericsson & Haswell (Eds.) (2006), Warschauer & Ware (2006), Dikli (2006 and 2007), and Chen & Cheng (2008) provides information on both the benefits of and the problems associated with using machines to assess student writing in-class, as well as for placement or other institutional purposes. Mostly, they (Chen & Cheng, 2008; Dikli, 2007; Warschauer & Grimes, 2008) claim that teachers need to intervene to help students translate the machine-provided feedback and incorporate it into their writing so it can be as useful as possible to them, but all note that more research into the different purposes of machine scoring is necessary.

It is crucial to understand the lens through which developers of automated essay scoring view writing and the assessment of writing. They focus on the perceived subjective nature of human scorers as well as the belief that reading and responding to student writing is a hardship on teachers. The word most often used by the industry to discuss this task is *burden,* or what Haswell (2006) refers to as "*drudgery*" (p. 57). Haswell (2006) is particularly tough on writing teachers when he claims, "We are complicit [in the drive to the use machines to score student writing]. We are where we are because for a very long time, we have been asking for it" (p. 59). And writing teachers *have* been asking for it, every time they whine about desks stacked with papers awaiting feedback. In fact, Jones (2006) reported that New Jersey K–12 teachers are interested in computer scoring specifically because they see it as alleviating their enormous grading loads Therefore, teachers need to know how machine scoring works, and they need to control the use of that technology in their classrooms. Further, teachers need to be aware, as Warschauer & Ware (2006) remind us, "The (AES) feedback varies in quality, but none of it is remotely similar to what a trained writing instructor can provide, and the ability of students to make use of the feedback is also questionable" (p. 160). Of course, students' ability to use feedback, no matter who (or what) gives it, is always problematic.

Ericsson & Haswell (2006) caution us about the pervasiveness of technology. Questioning why, even in the face of administrative decisions to use these scoring mechanisms, most educators remained uncharacteristically silent. Silence is often interpreted as tacit acceptance, which, they note, has allowed the industry to build energy, support, and enthusiasm that, if unchecked, could quickly result in the wholesale adoption of machine scoring.

Major Purveyors of Machine Scoring

Three main companies promote products that score essays—Educational Testing Services (ETS), Pearson Knowledge Technologies, and Vantage Learning/McCann Associates.

A thorough description of the technological details and the development of the software, scoring engines, and techniques used (natural language processing [NLP], latent semantic analysis [LSA], correlation, and artificial intelligence [AI]) are beyond the scope of this chapter; however, Dikli's (2006) excellent overview offers a detailed analysis of the current approaches to the machine scoring of essays. Other researchers provide in-depth analysis of various automated essay software engines, such as Project Essay Grade: PEG, (Page, 2003); Intellimetric ™ (Elliott 2003); Intelligent Essay Assessor (Landauer, Laham, & Foltz, 2000, 2003); and e-rater® (Burstein, 2003). This chapter presents a brief overview of how these programs work with an emphasis on the claims made by some of the major developers.

ETS's *e-rater* ®, a scoring engine, uses natural language processing (NLP), which can be described as a process that uses statistics, probability, and intelligent guessing. Burstein (2003) defines NLP as "the application of computational methods to analyze characteristics of electronic files of text or speech" (p. 115). *e-rater* ® is programmed to score essays "by analyzing large samples of essays on specific topics that have been calibrated by two or more expert readers" (ETS, 2007). The website is quick to point out that programs powered by *e-rater*® are designed to be used in conjunction with a writing teacher and are not meant to replace the writing teacher. ETS claims that *e-rater* ® performs feature analysis, model building, and content analysis based on vocabulary measures, text complexity/diction, proportion of grammar errors, proportion of usage errors, proportion of mechanics errors, proportion of style comments, organization and development score, and essay length, whose weight is explicitly controlled with a maximum of 30 percent (an attempt to downplay importance of essay length). It is interesting to note the disclaimer regarding essay length since some have reported a high correlation between essay length and high essay scores (Jones, 2006). Perelman (2005) found a correlation between length and a high score with the SAT writing test, claiming that he "could guess an essay's prescribed score just by looking at its length—even from across a room" (*Los Angeles Times,* May 29, 2005).

Pearson's Intelligent Essay Assessor (IEA) uses latent semantic analysis (LSA), which Landauer, Laham, & Foltz (2003) describe as "a machine learning method that acquires a mathematical representation of the meaning relations among words and passages by statistical computations applied to a large corpus of text" (p. 87). In other words, Landauer, Laham, & Foltz, the founders of Knowledge Analysis Technologies™ (KAT) and the developers of IEA who sold the KAT engine to Pearson Education in 2004 for an undisclosed sum (www.pearsonedmeasurement.com/news/6_29_04.htm), claim that IEA reads for *meaning.* Curious about how IEA might categorize meaning and provide understandable feedback, I found some text and submitted it. I received feedback that was, in my estimation, vague and unhelpful. I was told that I had written a very good first draft and to use the feedback provided to make my draft even better. My overall score (4 out of 6) was an average of scores in ideas (3), organization (3), conventions (4), sentence fluency (3), word choice (4), and voice (3). I was told that my writing demonstrated an inadequate ability to develop an effective organizational strategy, that my organization may not support my purpose, enhance my message, or move the reader through the text. I was instructed that my introduction was *either* missing, undeveloped, or predictable. Which was it? If IEA can read for meaning, surely it would know whether my introduction was missing or not. Or how might I develop my introduction better, if it was, in fact, undeveloped? I thought the machine would point to specific things in my essay, but the feedback was totally unspecific and seemed to generically address issues in any piece of writing, not the specific piece that I had submitted. I was given admonitions to make sure I introduced the reader to my topic and to create an attention-getting first impression that would make the reader want to finish reading what I'd written. I was then given a list of approaches to help me grab my reader's attention, basic attention getters such as describing a scenario, providing an unusual fact about the topic, including an appropriate quotation, or asking a rhetorical question. I was further instructed to make sure my thesis was clearly stated, that key ideas I used supported my thesis, that I presented supporting ideas as clearly and concisely as possible, and that I varied my sentence structure.

This feedback, while generally good, consisted mainly of generic comments rather than comments specifically tailored to my submission; the feedback was not specific enough to help me improve my writing and left many unanswered questions. Would second language writers know what a *scenario* is? *A* rhetorical question? How would a student interpret this feedback? Such imprecise feedback is both frustrating and unsupportive and certainly does not mimic the feedback that a student would receive from an experienced teacher during a writing conference.

IntelliMetric™, a Vantage Learning product, uses artificial intelligence (AI). However, Elliot (2003) calls IntelliMetric™ a "blend of artificial intelligence, natural language processing, and statistical technologies" (p. 71). IntelliMetric™ also "needs to be trained with a set of pre-scored essays with known scores assigned by human raters" (Dikli, 2006, p. 15). "These papers are used as a basis for the system to 'learn' the rubric and infer the pooled judgments of the human scorers. The

IntelliMetric™ system internalizes the characteristics of the responses associated with each score point and applies this intelligence to score essays with unknown scores" (Vantage Learning, 2005, p. 2). IntelliMetric™ claims to agree with or exceed expert human scoring; on average, IntelliMetric™ models claim to agree within one point of expert raters 97 to 100 percent of the time (Rudner, Garcia, & Welch, 2006).

Vantage Learning touts IntelliMetric™ as able to give meaningful feedback. In researching what computers focus on in an essay, however, Jones (2006) found that the College Board's placement product WritePlacer (which uses IntelliMetric™) doesn't notice differences in essays—quite an important notion for placement. Jones also found that WritePlacer places an exaggerated value on length, undervalues readability problems, and "appears to ignore the kinds of problems evinced by ESL students and even English speakers who have significant sentence-level problems" (Jones, 2006, p. 108).

All three of these powerful engines have instructional applications: Criterion℠ powered by ETS's e-rater®; WriteToLearn powered by Pearson's Intelligent Essay Assessor (IEA); and Vantage's MY Access!® powered by IntelliMetric™. Further, College Board and ACT use the IntelliMetric™ engine to run their online writing placement programs. Table 1 shows the claims made by these programs.

A Closer Look: MY Access!

In order to truly judge the effectiveness of these programs, let's take a closer look at one of them. MY Access!®, a Vantage Learning product powered by IntelliMetric®, is described as a "web-based instructional writing product that provides students enrolled in Grade 4 through higher education with the opportunity to develop their writing skills within an electronic portfolio-based environment" (Vantage Learning, 2007, p. 1). Teachers can select from more than 900 prompts in 5 genres (expository, informative, literary, narrative, and persuasive) or

TABLE 1: Instructional Applications of Machine Scoring Software

Program Name	Company	Scoring Engine/ Technique	Claims	Uses
ACCUPLACER WritePlacer ® Electronic and WritePlacer ® ESL	College Board	IntelliMetric ™ / artificial intelligence	Measures writing skill at the level expected of an entering level college student.	Placement into college-level composition classes for both L1 and L2
COMPASS e-write 2–8 e-write 2–12 ESL e-write	ACT	IntelliMetric™/ artificial intelligence	Maximizes the information postsecondary schools need to ensure student success; over 66% of ESL e-Write scores for the five analytic score domains match the raters' scores exactly.	Placement
CRITERION sm	ETS	e-rater ® / Natural Language Processing	Evaluates writing skills and provides score reporting and diagnostic feedback to instructors and students. Students draft and submit essays and receive immediate feedback in the form of a holistic score and diagnostic annotations within each essay that guide instruction.	In-class feedback, score reporting, and diagnostic feedback to instructors and students
My Access!	Vantage Learning	IntelliMetric ™ / artificial intelligence	Provides students with the practice they need to improve their writing skills. The program's powerful scoring engine grades students' essays instantly and provides targeted feedback, freeing teachers from grading thousands of papers by hand and giving them more time to conduct differentiated instruction and curriculum planning.	In-class writing
WriteToLearn	Pearson	Intelligent Essay Assessor (IEA) / latent semantic analysis	Provides easy-to-read reports to enable teachers to monitor class and individual progress; can help students improve reading comprehension and writing skills.	In-class writing skills and reading comprehension development tool

All **claims** are from the following corporate websites:
ACCUPLACER: www.collegeboard.com/highered/apr/accu/accu_wpp.html
COMPASS: www.act.org/e-write/index.html
CRITERION: www.ets.org/portal/site/ets/menuitem
WriteToLearn: www.writetolearn.net/Overview.html
My Access!: www.vantagelearning.com/myaccess/

create their own prompts. The program allows teachers to see students' online portfolios, which consist of original drafts, scores, revisions, comments from teachers, reflective journal entries, and IntelliMetric™ feedback. Further, MY Access!® recognizes typical L2 writing errors (B. Schweitzer, personal communication, November 14, 2007).

MY Access!® provides students with a variety of tools including a writing process guide, self-assessment rubrics, grammar feedback and rule explanation, word counter, genre-specific word banks, a spell-checker, and a variety of pre-writing tools. Students receive IntelliMetric™ feedback on either a 4- or 6-point holistic rubric assessing focus and meaning, organization, content and development, language use and style, and mechanics and conventions. Teachers can choose which rubric they would like to use.

Teachers have access to nine different reports including *student history,* which shows performance of one or more students over a period of time; *performance summary,* which shows the average performance overall (holistic score) and for each specific domain tested on one or more writing assignments; and *user frequency,* which provides information about how many students are writing to each prompt, as well as the performance of the students as a group for each prompt (Dikli, 2006; CLRN, 2007).

These reports may seem benign on the surface; however, closer analysis tells another story. Reports provide administrators with "numerical and graphical data to drive instruction, including NCLB compliant information and separate measurable objectives for all students and specific aggregated and disaggregated groups. School administrators can analyze data for all teachers and students in their school. MY Access!® enables school administrators to review student writing performance to more cost-effectively allocate professional development resources. District administrators can analyze performance of all schools within the district and use MY Access!® to achieve greater efficiencies in student performance monitoring while maintaining a high-quality instruction and assessment process" (CLRN, 2007). What can such data, when studied by administrators, mean for teachers? Might this data be used in a punitive fashion? In an age of accountability, if different cohorts of students can be compared, where might fault be found for performance considered less than adequate? With these questions in mind, the data might paint a rather solemn picture for teachers.

Vantage has done its homework, attempting to carefully situate MY Access!® in composition theory with a summary of writing instruction research. Vantage Learning contends, "Students need to have multiple opportunities to practice writing. Writing should be cross-curricular. Feedback regarding writing performance must be timely, and finally, writing instruction and assessment should incorporate clear learning objectives" (Vantage Learning, 2007, pp. 3–4). That MY Access!® is a product that can promote more student writing and revision is not the issue. Certainly it can. Additionally, the research behind the product has been carefully designed and implemented. Its use in formative assessment might be beneficial to many students.

However, the danger in programs such as MY Access!® is not that we *choose* to use them. The danger lies in *how* we use them. Possibly the most worrisome consequence might be the unintentional punitive effect on teachers. Will their use lead to greater *de-skilling* of teachers? *De-skilling* refers to teachers "who become simple deliverers of content and skill processes rather than those who intricately synthesize content, skills, and concepts to create sophisticated curriculum designed to meet the needs of their particular students" (Rice, n.d., p. 1). Instead of serving an additive function, might we one day use these programs in lieu of teachers? Will teachers be dismissed for results that do not meet administrative expectations? Are we setting ourselves up for teacher-less composition classes in the future? And what about the writing our students do? Ware (2006) cautions, "Particularly at the middle and high school levels, we often see savvy software programs swiftly and efficiently training students toward stilted, but well-organized, five-paragraph essays" (p. 135). By default, might we be instilling in our students an unintended definition of good writing?

Writing as Meaning Making

A very important consideration in the discussion of the machine scoring of essays is our reason for teaching composition. Especially in second language writing, some might believe that the mastery of a language should be a primary motive for teaching composition. In earlier days of L2 writing, this might have been the case. Teachers often used controlled writing (Leki, 1992) in the belief that student production of error would lead to fossilization of that error. Avoidance of error was key. In fact, Ross (1968) reminded teachers that control of sentence structure and accuracy in mechanics was basic to composition skill.

Today, however, teachers believe that collaboration and the social contexts associated with writing (Crowley, 1998) are important, and teachers eschew the notion of text as isolated artifact. That is, writing teachers, both L1 and L2 writing teachers, are concerned with *meaning making*—L2 teachers might refer to it as communicative competence, which entails much more than grammatical and mechanical correctness. Canale & Swain's (1980) canonical definition consists of four components: grammatical competence (words and rules), sociolinguistic competence (appropriateness), discourse competence (cohesion and coherence), and strategic competence (appropriate use of communication strategies). Writing is "a manifestation of, as well as the process of manifesting, sociolinguistic, strategic, and grammatical competences mediated by the use of orthographic systems" (Silva & Matsuda, 2002, p. 253).

If a firm is promoting the virtues of machine scoring of essays, it is critical to understand that program developer's definition of *meaning*. For example, how many of us share the belief of the developers of Intelligent Essay Assessor that "the fundamental idea is to think of a paragraph as an equation: its meaning equals a combination of the meaning of its words" (Landauer, Laham, & Foltz, 2003, p. 88)? This definition assumes that deciphering the meaning of a series of words is both necessary and sufficient to comprehend the meaning of a paragraph, essay, or story. That approach to essay scoring is reductive and naïve.

The fundamental question regarding machine scoring remains, are machines able to read for meaning? As previously mentioned, some machine-scoring promoters (particularly Intelligent Essay Assessor [IEA]) advertise their products as able to ascertain meaning (Ericsson & Haswell, 2006). IEA does this by comparing the submission to a set of essays previously read and rated by humans. However, defining meaning itself can be elusive. We cannot assume that test developers, psychometricians, cognitive psychologists, and computer scientists define meaning in the same way, or that they individually or collectively use similar standards to evaluate meaning, as do teachers of writing. Defining the meaning of meaning is vital if we are to critically evaluate claims that specific programs can ascertain meaning. Ericsson (2006) reminds us that when "Vantage Learning's promotional material defines 'focus and meaning' as 'cohesiveness and consistency in purpose and main idea; maintaining a single point of view,' we must assume that their understanding of meaning is somehow encompassed in those fourteen words and that their technologies depend on this simplistic definition" (p. 30). Another issue, especially with L2 writers in particular, is whether machine scoring can adjust for nonstandard, nontarget uses of the language or whether it will be confounded or misled by them.

Positive Views

Those in support of the machine scoring of essays believe that scoring engines such as *e-rater* ®, IntelliMetric™, and Intelligent Essay Assessor™ are useful for large-scale assessments of writing. Many standardized writing tests have adopted the machine scoring of essays; in fact, in January 2007, Vantage Learning announced that IntelliMetric™ would score the writing section of the Medical College Admission Test (MCAT).

Some programs might be useful in the classroom as supplemental to or as an extension of teacher feedback. Bereiter (2003) states that the technology "ought to be able to overcome the human foibles" (p. vii), such as the halo effect. Shermis & Burstein (2003) believe that machine scoring may predict as well as humans, that it correlates well with human behavior, and that it possesses a high degree of construct validity.

And again, supporters cite the benefit of increased feedback to students who want to write more than teachers can read. I question the existence of such students, but if they do, in fact, exist, the overworked teacher, buried under mountains of papers, could use MY Access!® to solve this problem, encouraging students to write as much as they want and get immediate feedback. This is, in fact, the strongest argument for online scoring programs but only if one believes that the teacher is the only possible or legitimate respondent; if other respondents (peer, self) are utilized, that argument quickly loses strength. Other benefits, according to product purveyors, include instant scoring, increased student motivation to write, and the idea that the programs are risk free and self-paced.

Besides those benefits, the big three (see the table on page 168) consistently claim that electronic scoring is:

- fast—the samples are scored and the reports produced within seconds to allow immediate feedback and advising.
- reliable—research demonstrates close agreement between electronically generated scores and those assigned by expert human raters.
- affordable—especially when compared to the cost of hand-scoring essays.

Negative Views

Before integrating any new teaching tool into their pedagogies, teachers should carefully evaluate the costs, financial and otherwise, associated with that integration. The covert costs involved with the integration of programs that machine score students' writing are high. Condon (2006) cites the loss of local control, the loss of the human element that contributes to professional development and writing program cohesion, and the inherent limitations of a short, timed writing exam.

Rothermel (2006) asserts that machine scoring companies, MY Access!® in particular, show contempt for classroom teachers, especially those working in primary and secondary grades. She sees their ideology as one "that defines not just writing, but also teaching and learning, as formulaic and asocial endeavors" (p. 200). She further contends that MY Access!® "narrows the learning environment" (p. 204). Dikli (2006) reports that while Criterion℠, MY Access! ®, and IntelliMetric™ possess the capacity for multilingual feedback, she questions how their "current practices address the needs of ELL students" (p. 24) and calls for investigations that examine the appropriateness of the "style content, and amount of feedback . . . for the ELL population" (p. 24). Once again, can a machine adapt to the nonstandard language sometimes produced by a second language writer?

Those who take a less favorable view of the machine scoring of essays caution that the machines do what they are programmed to do and thus lack a sense of the writer and/or rater as a person (Hamp-Lyons, 2001) and cannot really appreciate an essay as human readers do (Page, 2003).

When the benefits of machine scoring programs are discussed, little mention is made of the fact that in these programs, writing is constructed as an individual activity, disregarding the social interaction of writing. Additionally, essays are based on norms and become displays of skill. There is an emphasis on grammar, usage, and organization. Displacement of teacher authority is evident. McGee (2006) demonstrated that the kind of language analysis embedded in Intelligent Essay Assessor "cannot be trusted to score student essays well" (p. 92) and that automated essay scoring does not provide meaningful evaluation.

Professional Claims

The CCCC has published two position statements outlining its perspective regarding the machine scoring of essays. The first, in the *CCCC Position Statement on Teaching, Learn-*

ing, and Assessing Writing in Digital Environments (CCCC, 2004), is titled *A Current Challenge: Electronic Rating*. In the statement, we are reminded of the social nature of writing and the need for writing to be scored by readers, no matter the purpose for writing. The statement lists disadvantages to machine scoring, including the violation of the social nature of writing. Further, writing to a machine sends an inappropriate message to students about the value our institutions place on writing and lessens the validity of the assessment. Additionally, high schools will begin preparing their students to write to a machine if colleges begin to use machine scoring. CCCC concludes its position statement by clearly opposing machine-scored writing.

Again in 2006, CCCC addressed this issue in *Writing Assessment: A Position Statement* (CCCC, 2006). The statement summarizes best practices for writing assessment. The Committee set down five guiding principles for the assessment of writing. Principle two reads: "Writing is by definition social. Learning to write entails learning to accomplish a range of purposes for a range of audiences in a range of settings. Therefore best assessment practice is direct assessment by human readers." The statement further reminds us that "automated assessment programs do not respond as human readers. While they may promise consistency, they distort the very nature of writing as a complex and context-rich interaction between people. They simplify writing in ways that can mislead writers to focus more on structure and grammar than on what they are saying by using a given structure and style" (CCCC, 2006).

Clearly, the CCCC Committee on Assessment understands the need for locally developed assessments specified by assessment scholars (Condon, 2006; Crusan, 2003, 2006, 2010; Hamp-Lyons, 2001, 2002, 2003; Haswell, 2006; Huot, 2002; Weigle, 2002; White, 1994, 1995, 1996a, 2001). All assessment, whatever the purpose, should be locally developed by those who teach writing, with a very particular context as its target, and should be read and scored by readers familiar with the context.

Truth and Consequences

Intrinsically, writing is complex and variable, challenging any agreed on definition of the construct. As a result of this complex variability, it is difficult to imagine assessing the writing of L2 writers impartially and reliably because this population embodies nearly every potential variation (Cumming, 2002). How then might a machine define "good writing" in addition to noticing, accounting for, understanding, and fairly assessing this variability?

As noted earlier, although the pool is expanding, little research presently exists regarding the effects that using a computer to evaluate writing has on second language writers. One of the few current studies, Dikli's 2007 dissertation, explores how ESL students incorporated the feedback they received either from an AES system or from the teacher in their writings. Among other things, Dikli found that the instant scoring function of MY Access!® motivated students to write more; however, Dikli reported one teacher's reaction as follows:

> I think it might be used once every couple of weeks just to get them into something different. I just don't think it is better or as good as human feedback. Encouragement, looking into nuances, the whole [teacher/student] interaction is missing. (p. 307)

While we certainly are not able to generalize from one teacher's reaction, we might guess that this response could be common among writing teachers.

How might computerized essay grading be especially harmful for second language writers? Matzen & Sorensen (2006) conducted a pilot study investigating e-Write, ACT's computer-based writing essay test; they wondered if e-Write would accurately score timed placement essays. Although ACT creates expectations of high correlations between the scores generated by e-Write and human raters, Matzen & Sorensen (2006) reported only a .56 correlation—the closer the number is to +1 or –1, the more closely the two variables are related—and concluded, first, that "the rater scores have greater criterion-related validity, and second, the e-Write scores would have resulted in a substantial misplacement of students" (p. 136). This can be particularly true for L2 learners who may have uneven profiles of performance across different aspects of writing (Weigle, 2002).

Chodorow & Burstein (2004) evaluated e-rater's performance on TOEFL® essays. They examined the relationship between essay length and holistic scores assigned to essays by e-rater®, the automated essay scoring system developed by ETS. They found that a newer version of e-rater® performs significantly better than its predecessor and is less dependent on length due to its greater reliance on measures of topical content and on the complexity and diversity of vocabulary. Their goal for future work is "to make available an even larger and more sophisticated array of features. Not only will this lead to better scoring performance, but it will also let us capture more of the richness and diversity of human language" (p. 31). Chodorow is professor of Psychology at Hunter College, CUNY; Burstein is principal development scientist at ETS.

Warschauer & Ware (2006) have found through observation that teachers use automated writing evaluation (AWE) software in many ways, from encouraging submission of multiple drafts from their students to using software to simulate high-stakes writing assessments. However, they nurse a healthy skepticism for machine scoring, adding that not enough is known about its effects to make an informed decision. They define the classroom research agenda, calling for "well-designed product-, process-, and product/process studies of AWE use in the classroom" (p. 176). They conclude, "We believe that . . . technology that empowers by providing instant evaluation and feedback, and technology that dehumanizes by eliminating the human element exist in automated writing evaluation software" (p. 176). They call for more experimental examination into the ways the software is used in classrooms to determine whether it empowers or dehumanizes, and to what degree.

As it stands now, particularly for writing teachers, the division between those who favor the use of machine scoring and those who do not still exists. Many teachers view machine scoring negatively. We are reminded (Cumming, 2007; Haswell, 2006) of our complacency where the machine scoring of essays is concerned, having been content to criticize from afar without really understanding, maybe hoping that it will go away. But technology is here to stay, and so examination of these issues by our field is imperative (Cumming, 2007; Dikli, 2006, 2007; Haswell, 2006; Warschauer & Grimes, 2008; Warschauer & Ware, 2006). There is clearly a need to examine the implementations, implications, and impact of machine scoring. Chastising our "polemic about resistance" (Cumming, 2007, p. 82) in regard to machine scoring, Cumming adds that this diatribe is largely ineffectual. What we really need to do is what Haswell (2006) suggests: accept that assessment is our job and that it is difficult, for if we do not, "easy evaluation (in the form of machine scoring) will drive out good evaluation every time" (p. 78). Additionally, we need to fashion coherent, rational, and data-based arguments in our decision to use (or not) machines to score the writing of our students.

It should be clear that machines that score students' writing, if used at all, ought to be used with care and constant teacher supervision and intervention. Presently, no clear evidence exists that machine scoring programs are able to handle the diversity of language produced by second language writers. I have seen L2 writers become very frustrated when faced with overwhelming feedback, especially on nonstandard language use. In fact, when I train writing teachers, I am quick to remind them that when providing direct feedback, they should concentrate on a few of the most grievous errors at a time, thereby not overwhelming their student writers. Further, teachers should inform their students prior to writing what aspects the teacher will focus on for that particular piece of writing.

This technology is here to stay. Even as I write this, researchers are quickly moving this technology forward, creating more powerful programs and more sophisticated programs. As a result, teachers must understand this technology and strive to keep assessments locally controlled, context-specific, and accessible.

Suggestions for Teachers

1. Explore the Internet sites of computerized/online essay scoring systems. Some of the most notable are:
   Criterion: http://criterion28.ets.org/cwe/
   e-write: www.act.org/e-write/index.html
   WriteToLearn: www.writetolearn.net/
   MY Access!: www.gomyaccess.com/myaccess/do/log
   In groups, compare the sites in reference to services, prices, and delivery options. What promises are made on these websites?
2. Write a letter responding to an administration's call for the use of machines to score essays to be used for admissions to a university, or to a school district's decision for the wholesale adoption of any computerized/online essay scoring system.

Suggestions for Further Reading

To be more informed about the inner workings and science behind machine scoring, see Mark Shermis & Jill Burstein's 2003 edited collection *Automated Essay Scoring: A Cross-Disciplinary Perspective.*

For a look at institutional uses of machine scoring, their outcomes, and a political perspective, see Patricia Ericsson & Richard Haswell's 2006 edited collection *Machine Scoring of Essays: Truth and Consequences.*

Epilogue: Where Do We Go from Here?

Progress lies not in enhancing what is, but in advancing toward what will be.
—Kahlil Gibran

In 1996, Hamp-Lyons & Kroll claimed, "We understand a great deal less about our test-takers from countries around the world than we need to: This is the great underresearched aspect of language testing" (p. 236). I imagine that we still understand far less than we need to, that we have only scratched the surface in our understanding of second language writing and writing assessment. The questions we have today about how best to assess writing will most assuredly still be on the minds of teachers in decades to come. As we move further into the 21st century, some of the major concerns in L2 writing assessment will include the burgeoning ELL population in the United States, the growing use of English as a lingua franca around the world, how to provide better and more widespread teacher training in assessment, the uses of technology for assessment, and, of course, large-scale assessment/accountability.

ELL Population in the United States

To say that the English language learner population is growing is an understatement. Statistics for this growing population border on the amazing. In South Carolina, the ELL population has grown by 714 percent since 1994–1995 (Payan & Nettles, 2008). Payan and Nettles supply statistics for other states: Kentucky's population is up by 417.4 percent; Indiana's by 407.8 percent; and Pennsylvania's by 100.3 percent. Clearly, English language learners are the fastest growing population in U.S. schools today.

Despite this exploding ELL population, many teachers still do not recognize the presence of L2 writers in their classroom (Ferris, Brown, Collins, Liu, & Stine, 2009). Still others are hesitant to admit their presence either because they are unsure about how to teach them or they feel that since they are not trained language teachers they should not have L2 students in their classrooms. Some teachers are adamant about this. However, it is not appropriate or acceptable for teachers to deny the presence of ELLs or for ELLs to be removed from their care. We must rise to the challenge to better serve this rapidly growing population in the classroom. Teachers need to accept the challenge and prepare themselves and modify their pedagogy to better accommodate these students. All educators should be prepared to help students learn both English and academic content. This may translate into additional education for many teachers so that they can understand the processes involved in language acquisition. Teachers also need to know how to identify ELLs, how to get authentic assessments of their abilities, and how to adapt materials. These are large requirements and will require preparation and dedication on the part of both teachers and teacher training programs.

Teacher Training

Many teachers are not formally trained to teach writing (Crusan, 2004) and are often even less ready to assess it. Weigle (2007) claims that although writing teachers must assess writing, an assessment course is often not mandatory. She further maintains that even when writing pedagogy courses are taken, the classes often include only a limited discussion of the practical applications of assessment. When teachers are unprepared to assess writing, they often fall back on assessing writing errors because they often feel it is safe ground. Teachers can attend to errors in lieu of assessing issues for which they have limited or no training. Those who supervise teacher training programs need to ensure that our programs require the necessary courses to train teachers in all the skills necessary for classroom teaching, including assessing writing (and other skills). (See the 2009 CCCC Statement on Second Language Writing and Writers.)

Another issue in teacher training concerns the lack of training of K–12 teachers in all aspects of language acquisition and the needs of ELLs. Because the population of ELLs is growing so quickly, teacher training programs in colleges of education and state departments need to make certain that prospective and practicing teachers are prepared to deal with language issues as well as cultural and socioeconomic issues.

Additionally, more collaboration is necessary between teachers of high school English and ESL and college L1 and L2 writing instructors. Collaborative initiatives promote mutual respect as well as education—all parties have much to teach and much to learn from each other. Further, at the university level, writing across the curriculum (WAC) programs should encourage faculty to take writing assessment workshops.

The Uses of Technology for Assessment

For good or ill, technology is here to stay. New technologies are constantly pushing the technological envelope forward. Ten years ago, I would never have thought I would be teaching a class online. Today, I conduct meetings with colleagues on Skype™, hold virtual office hours via email, and teach using Elluminate®. I use the text messaging feature of my cell phone daily to communicate with family and friends; while at professional conferences, text messaging helps me locate colleagues at meetings, for both business meetings and social engagements. When I witness the long lines of people waiting to use computers at conferences I generally attend, it is clear to me that language teachers use and depend on technology. We have arrived in a brave new virtual world.

Technology reaches everywhere and affects students, teachers, and our workload. While most institutions of higher education make extensive use of technology, teachers in the K–12 environment may not have access to technology generally afforded university faculty, perhaps resulting in the uneven education of students, since some students come to the university with limited or spotty experience with technology. Therefore, we need to be careful in our assumptions about the technological experience of our students. Having said that, I have seen very recent Iraqi immigrant high school students (in the United States for one month) with email accounts, Facebook® pages, and the ability to navigate YouTube.

Technology can ease or cause problems. Because of our dependence on technology, we sometimes experience hardship or annoyance when, due to a computer glitch or operator error, we lose what we have been writing or when our students sit in our classes with faces glued to their laptop screens. Are they taking notes or checking their Facebook® page? With trepidation, I have had to ask students on some occasions to close their laptops and engage with class material in real time. Additionally, I have seen teacher workload increase with every new advance in technology. Because email is instantaneous, I have occasionally experienced some impatience on the part of students. The rapidity with which messages reach us often makes us believe that our answer should be just as rapid. So married are we to every new gadget that I often wonder if technology has succeeded in putting our society on an electronic leash.

Another technology, the machine scoring of writing, has its own set of concerns for teachers. Both writing teachers and assessment specialists should be calling for critical evaluation of the suitability and reliability of this technology. Companies promoting this technology make claims that necessitate careful discussion and independent research before educators adopt this technology for use in the classroom or for scoring writing on standardized tests. It is critical that composition and assessment specialists conduct more research on the influence of every technology that impacts writing assessment.

Large-Scale Assessment/Accountability

The financial, emotional, and professional costs of the current accountability system are too high. Often, students, teachers, and school districts are held accountable for test scores despite having to teach under poor conditions. In the United States, school systems are not, but should be, equally funded. ELLs generally attend schools in lower socioeconomic areas; they often receive less than adequate education due in part to suboptimal surroundings, have little access to technology, and are given teaching materials that are frequently outdated. Until school systems are funded equally, these appalling conditions will remain. So I raise these questions:

- Isn't a measure of a nation's integrity how it treats its most vulnerable—the children and the poor?
- What would a just accountability system look like?
- How can we guarantee fairness for all?

Clearly the commercialism of accountability—monopolized by (mostly) large for-profit organizations—has failed to provide a just solution. If standardized tests could solve the problems in education, the problems would already have been solved—by one teacher's account (Monroe, 2006) his students "missed 33 days of ESL classes, or about 18 percent of their English instruction, due to standardized testing" (p. 1).

Finally, we need to concern ourselves with the rapid move to bring a No Child Left Behind accountability to the university. While accountability is certainly not bad, we need to be cautious about the purposes for which standardized tests are used at the university. How will they affect what is taught? An even more critical question—how will they affect the academic freedom of university professors? Freedom of inquiry is an essential component of the work of academics, for both themselves and their students. Will the introduction of a test to determine what students have learned during their college education restrict the freedom and flow of ideas traditionally the bastion of the American university?

Final Thoughts

Scholars [Huot (2002), McNamara & Roever (2006), O'Neill, Moore, & Huot (2009), White (2001)] again and again refer to the gap between those who work in the field of psychometrics and those who primarily work in the classroom at levels from K–16. McNamara & Roever (2006) call for the "breakdown of the disciplinary walls between language testing researchers and those working within other areas of applied linguistics, social science, and the humanities generally" (p. 254). On the other hand, Petruzzi (2008) calls us to fight "the pervasive presence of scientism in writing assessment" (p. 239). He argues that "we are not 'measuring' writing as scientists; rather, we are humanists analyzing the thinking and reasoning—equally hermeneutic and rhetorical performances—of other human beings" (p. 254). Clearly, in Petruzzi's estimation, the line between human and machine is still drawn.

Where we are headed in writing assessment has been determined, in large part, by where we have been. The trends have been explored in a variety of contexts in this book. The future appears bleak but is not hopeless. Teachers must regain control of assessment. This book provides the background information, tools, and logical arguments for the empowerment of writing teachers to regain a role in shaping their destiny in particular and the destiny of the field of writing assessment in general.

Appendix 1

Self-Assessment Letter for the Argumentative Essay

You will write a 1 to 1.5 page self-assessment letter. In this letter, you will evaluate your argumentative essay. Your letter should be typed, double-spaced, and in 11-point Arial font. Below is a sample format to follow when writing your letter.

04/22/10

Dear Student A,

Xxxxxxxxxxxxxxxxxxxxxxxxxxxxxxxxxxxxxx. Xxxxxxxxxxxxxxxxxxxxxxxxxxxxxxx. Xxxxxxxxxxxxxxxxxxxxxxxxxxxxxxxxxxxxxxx.

Xxxxxxxxxxxxxxxxxxxxxx. Xxxxxxxxxxxxxxxxxxxxxxxxxxxxxxxxxxxxxxxxxxxx. Xxxxxxxxxxxxxxxxxxxxxxxxxxxxxxxxxxxxxxxxxxxxxxxxxxxxxxxxxxxxxxxxxxxxxx.

Xxxxxxxxxxxxxxxxxxxxxxxxxxx. Xxxxxxxxxxxxxxxxxxxxxxxxxxxxxxxxxxxx. Xxxxxxxxxxxxxxxxxxxxxxxxxxxxx.

Sincerely,
Student B

When writing your letter, refer to the criteria on the next page. Your letter should have an introduction and conclusion. All body paragraphs should relate to your thesis statement. You must give specific examples from your argumentative essay when discussing it in your letter.

*Below is an example of how to use quotes from your essay in your self-assessment letter.

In my argumentative essay, my thesis statement is very strong. At first, it was not very specific, so I revised it a few times. Now, my thesis statement is much more specific. It states, "Poverty is a growing problem in our world, and to help solve this problem, we should increase our funding for welfare." In my first draft of this essay, my thesis did not discuss a clear solution to the problem. I had not narrowed my focus yet, so I revised my thesis to discuss one particular solution that I think will solve the problem of poverty.

*You can also paraphrase in your letter.

My thesis statement is not as strong as I would have liked it to be. I had a hard time being specific. My thesis statement discusses how setting more money aside for welfare will help people in poverty. However, I do not think this is specific enough. I should have also discussed how much we should increase the funding for welfare and why this would be a good solution.

How you will be evaluated:

Criteria	Strong	Good	Adequate	Weak
Format: The letter is 1 to 1.5 pages typed and double-spaced. It must be formatted like a letter. Each paragraph is indented. The letter has 1-inch margins and 11-point Arial font.	1	1	1	0
Introduction: Introduces the topic. The last sentence should be like a thesis statement, letting readers know what your letter will discuss.	3	2.5	2	1
Body: Discusses strengths in your argumentative essay. Gives specific examples of these.	4	3	2	1
Discusses things that could be improved in your essay. (These will be your weaknesses.) Gives specific examples of these.	4	3	2	1
Discusses what you've learned from writing this essay. Gives specific examples of these.	4	3	2	1
All paragraphs have clear topic sentences. All ideas in the paragraph support the topic sentence.	3	2.5	2	1
Each paragraph includes specific examples from your essay. (You can use quotes from your argumentative essay or paraphrase ideas from your essay.)	3	2.5	2	1
Conclusion: Summarizes your letter. Refers to your thesis statement.	3	2.5	2	1
Vocabulary: The letter uses an appropriate range of vocabulary.	2	1.5	1	0
Grammar: The letter has been proofread and has few grammar errors.	3	2	1	0
Total:	/30			

Brainstorming for Self-Assessment Letter

On a separate piece of paper, answer these questions. Thinking of these answers will help you to prepare for your self-assessment letter. You don't have to answer every single question. Think about which ones are most important to you.

1. What **new skills** have you discussed in class while writing your argumentative essay?

   The big parts of an essay:
   What have you learned about writing introductions?
   What have you learned about writing conclusions?
   What have you learned about creating a focus for an essay?
   What have you learned about structuring paragraphs?
   What have you learned about cohesion and organization in an essay?

   The smaller parts of an essay:
   What have you learned about transitions?
   What have you learned about vocabulary in writing?
   What have you learned about sentence types?
   What have you learned about grammar?
   What did you learn about paraphrasing and quoting?
   What have you learned about using APA format?

   Before writing the essay:
   What have you learned about doing research?
   How did you do the research for this essay?
   What did you learn about adding someone else's ideas to your own ideas?
   What reading strategies did you use when doing research?
   What other new writing skills have you discussed in class?

2. What are some of your **strengths** in your argumentative essay?

   Think about the questions above. Which of those did you do really well?

3. What are some of your **weaknesses** in this essay?

Again, think about the questions above. Which of those do you struggle with? Where can you improve? What would you still revise in your essay if you could?

From Trisha Folck & Emily Franklin, Wright State University ESL writing instructors

References

ACT. (2008). *ACT writing test: Validity studies.* Retrieved December 17, 2008, from www.act.org/aap/writing/sample/index.html

———. (2008). *ACT writing test: Writing test scores.* Retrieved December 29, 2008, from www.act.org/aap/writing/sample/rubric.html

———. (2008). *The ACT writing test.* Retrieved November 19, 2008, from www.act.org/aap/writing/index.html

Bachman, L. F., & Palmer, A. S. (1996). *Language testing in practice: Designing and developing useful language tests.* Oxford: Oxford University Press.

Belanoff, P. (1991). The myths of assessment. *Journal of Basic Writing, 1*(1), 54–66.

Bereiter, C. (2003). Foreword. In M. D. Shermis & J. C Burstein (Eds.). *Automated essay scoring: A cross-disciplinary perspective* (pp. vii–ix). Mahwah, NJ: Lawrence Erlbaum.

Bergmann, A., Hall K. C., & Ross, S. M. (Eds.). (2007). *Language files: Materials for an introduction to language and linguistics* (10th ed.). Columbus: Ohio State University Press.

Berlin, J. A. (1987). *Rhetoric and reality: Writing instruction in American colleges, 1900–1985.* Carbondale: Southern Illinois University Press.

Blake, R. J. (2008). *Brave new digital classroom: Technology and foreign language learning.* Washington, DC: Georgetown University Press.

Bloch, J. (2008). *Technologies in the second language composition classroom.* Ann Arbor: University of Michigan Press.

Bourdieu, P. (1996). *The rules of art: Genesis and structure of the literary field.* Palo Alto, CA: Stanford University Press.

———. (2005). *The social structure of the economy.* Cambridge, UK: Polity Press.

Brandon, K. (2002). Test-prep pressure hits the schools. In A. Kohn & P. Shannon (Eds.), *Education, Inc: Turning learning into business* (revised edition) (pp. 58–62). Portsmouth, NH: Heinemann.

Breland, H. M. (1996). Computer-assisted writing assessment: The politics of science versus the humanities. In E. M. White, W. D. Lutz, & S. Kamusikiri (Eds.), *Assessment of writing: Politics, policies, practices* (pp. 249–256). New York: Modern Language Association of America.

Britton, J., Burgess, T., Martin, N., McLeod, A., & Rosen, H. (1975). The process of writing. In *The development of writing abilities* (pp. 19–49). London: Macmillan.

Broad, B. (2003). *What we really value: Beyond rubrics in teaching and assessing writing.* Logan: Utah State University Press.

———. (2006). More work for teachers? Possible futures of teaching writing in the age of computerized assessment. In P. F. Ericsson & R. Haswell (Eds.), *Machine scoring of essays: Truth and consequences* (pp. 221–233). Logan: Utah University Press.

Brown, H. D. (2004). *Language assessment: Principles and classroom practices.* White Plains, NY: Pearson Education, Inc.

Bullock, R. (1991). Autonomy and community in the evaluation of writing. In R. Bullock & J. Trimbur (Eds.), *The politics of writing instruction: Postsecondary* (pp. 191–205). Portsmouth, NH: Boynton/Cook.

Burstein, J. (2003). The e-rater engine: Automated essay scoring with natural language processing. In M. D. Shermis & J. C. Burstein (Eds.), *Automated essay scoring: A cross-disciplinary perspective* (pp. 113–121). Mahwah, NJ: Lawrence Erlbaum.

Burstein, J., Chodorow, M., & Leacock, C. (2004). Automated essay evaluation: The criterion online writing service. *AI Magazine*, 27–36.

California Learning Resource Network (CLRN). (2007). *Electronic Learning Assessment Resources: MY Access!®*. Retrieved November 24, 2007, from www.clrn.org/elar/details.cfm?elarid=16

Callahan, S. (1995). Portfolio expectations: Possibilities and limits. *Assessing Writing, 2*(2), 117–151.

Canale, M., & Swain, M. (1980). Theoretical bases of communicative approaches to second language teaching and testing. *Applied Linguistics, 1*, 1–47.

Carroll, L. A. (2003). *Rehearsing new roles: How college students develop as writers.* Carbondale: Southern Illinois University Press.

Casanave, C. P. (2004). *Controversies in second language writing: Dilemmas and decisions in research and instruction*. Ann Arbor: University of Michigan Press.

CCCC Committee on Assessment. (1995). Writing assessment: A position statement. *College Composition and Communication, 46*(1), 430–437.

———. (2004). *CCCC position statement on teaching, learning, and assessing writing in digital environments*. Retrieved January 10, 2007, from www.ncte.org/cccc/resources/positions

———. (2006). *Writing assessment: A position statement*. Retrieved July 23 2007, from www.ncte.org/cccc/resources/positions/writingassessment

CCCC Committee on Second Language Writing. (2009, November). *CCCC statement on second language writing and writers*. Retrieved April 2, 2010, from www.ncte.org/cccc/resources/positions/secondlangwriting

Chen, C-F. E., & Cheng, W-Y. E. (2008). Beyond the design of automated writing evaluation: Pedagogical practices and perceived learning effectiveness in EFL writing classes. *Language Learning & Technology, 12*(2), 94–112.

Chodorow, M., & Burstein, J. (2004). Beyond essay length: Evaluating e-rater's performance on TOEFL essays (TOEFL Research Rep. No. RR-73, ETS RR-04-04). Princeton, NJ: ETS. Retrieved September 15, 2007, from www.ets.org/portal/site/ets/menuitem

Cizek, G. J., & Page, B. A. (2003). The concept of reliability in the context of automated essay scoring. In M. D. Shermis & J. C. Burstein (Eds.), *Automated essay scoring: A cross-disciplinary perspective* (pp. 125–145). Mahwah, NJ: Lawrence Erlbaum.

Cole, P. (2005, May 3). SAT essay has schools buffing rusted writing skills (Update 1). *Bloomberg.com*. Retrieved May 16, 2005, from www.bloomberg.com

College Board. (2008). *College admission – SAT & SAT subject tests*. www.collegeboard.com/student/testing/sat/about.html

Condon, W. (2006). Why less is not more: What we lose by letting a computer score writing samples. In P. F. Ericsson & R. Haswell (Eds.), *Machine scoring of essays: Truth and consequences* (pp. 211–220). Logan: Utah University Press.

Connors, R. J. (1990). Rhetoric in the modern university: The creation of an underclass. In R. Bullock & J. Trimbur (Eds.), *The politics of writing assessment: Postsecondary* (pp. 55–84). Portsmouth, NH: Boynton/Cook.

Connor, U. (1996). *Contrastive rhetoric: Cross-cultural aspects of second-language writing.* New York: Cambridge University Press.

———. (2003). Changing currents in contrastive rhetoric: Implications for teaching and research. In B. Kroll (Ed.), *Exploring the dynamics of second language writing* (pp. 218–241). New York: Cambridge University Press.

Cooper, P. L. (1984). *The assessment of writing ability: A review of research* (No. ED250332). Bloomington, IN: ERIC Clearinghouse on Reading and Communication Skills.

Craddock, C. (2009). Harry Potter and first-year writing, or, where online fan activities intersect with brick-and-mortar institutions. *The Fogdog Review* (Fall 2008/Winter 2009), 5–16.

Crowley, S. (1990). *The methodical memory: Invention in current-traditional rhetoric.* Carbondale: Southern Illinois University Press.

———. (1996). Response to Edward M. White. *Journal of Basic Writing, 15*(1), 88–91.

———. (1998). *Composition in the university: Historical and polemical essays.* Pittsburgh: University of Pittsburgh Press.

Crusan, D. (2001, March). *Conflicting communities: ESL writers and disharmonious definitions of academic discourse.* Paper presented at the 52nd Annual Convention – College Conference on Composition and Communication, Denver, CO.

———. (2002a). An assessment of ESL writing placement assessment. *Assessing Writing: An International Journal, 8*, 17–30.

———. (2002b). The quagmire of assessment for placement: Talking out of both sides of our mouths. *TESL Reporter, 35*(2), 37–48.

———. (2003). The persistence of indirect assessment for placement and its effects on ESL writers. *TESOL in Action, 17*(1), 13–15.

———. (2004). *Preparing teachers of second language writing.* Paper presented at the 38th Annual TESOL Convention and Exposition, Long Beach, CA.

———. (2006). The politics of implementing online directed self-placement for second language writers. In P. K. Matsuda, C. Ortmeier-Hooper, & X. You (Eds.), *The politics of second language writing* (pp. 205–221). West Lafayette, IN: Parlor Press.

———. (2010). Assess thyself lest others assess thee. In T. Silva & P. K. Matsuda (Eds.), *Practicing theory in second language writing* (pp. 245–262). West Lafayette, IN: Parlor Press.

Crusan, D., & Cornett, C. (2002). The cart before the horse: Teaching assessment criteria before writing. *The International Journal for Teachers of English Writing Skills, 9,* 20–33.

Cumming, A. (2002). Assessing L2 writing: Alternative constructs and ethical dilemmas. *Assessing Writing, 8*, 73–83.

———. (2007). Book Review. [Review of the book *Machine Scoring of Student Essays: Truth and Consequences*]. *Assessing Writing, 12*, 80–82.

de Cohen, C. C., & Clewell, B. C. (2007). *Putting English language learners on the educational map: The No Child Left Behind act implemented.* Education in Focus: Urban Institute Policy Brief ED498664. Retrieved January 23, 2008, from www.eric.ed.gov

Delpit, L. D. (1988). The silenced dialogue: Power and pedagogy in educating other people's children. *Harvard Educational Review, 58*(3), 280–298.

———. (2006). *Other people's children: Cultural conflict in the classroom.* New York: New Press.

Dikli, S. (2006). An overview of automated scoring of essays. *Journal of Technology, Learning, and Assessment, 5*(1). Retrieved November 29, 2006, from www.jtla.org

———. (2007). *Automated essay scoring in an ESL setting.* Unpublished doctoral dissertation, Florida State University, Tallahassee.

Dubois, P. H. (1970). *A history of psychological testing.* Boston: Allyn & Bacon.

Educational Marketer. (October 8, 2001). *Publishers suffer growing pains as testing market mushrooms, 32*(29), 4–6.

Edumetry. (2008). *Rich feedback: Learning, retention, success.* Retrieved March 30, 2008, from www.richfeedback.com/index.html

Elbow, P., & Belanoff, P. (1997). Reflections on an explosion: Portfolios in the 90s and beyond. In K. Yancey & I. Weiser (Eds.), *Situating portfolios: Four perspectives* (pp. 21–33). Logan: Utah State University Press.

Elliot, N. (2005). *On a scale: A social history of writing assessment.* New York: Peter Lang.

Elliot, N., Plata, M., & Zelhart, P. (1990). *A program development handbook for the holistic assessment of writing.* Lanham, MD: University Press of America, Inc.

Elliot, S. (2003). IntelliMetric: from here to validity. In Mark D. Shermis and Jill C. Burstein (Eds.). *Automated essay scoring: A cross disciplinary approach.* Mahwah, NJ: Lawrence Erlbaum.

Emery, K., & Ohanian, S. (2004). *Why is corporate America bashing our public schools?* Portsmouth, NH: Heinemann.

Emig, J. (1971). *The composing processes of twelfth graders.* Urbana, IL: National Council of Teachers of English.

Englert, C. S., Manalo, M., & Zhao, Y. (2004). I can do it better on the computer: The effects of technology-enabled scaffolding on young writers' composition. *Journal of Special Education Technology, 19*(1), 5–22.

Ericsson, P. F. (2006). The meaning of meaning: Is a paragraph more than an equation? In P. F. Ericsson & R. H. Haswell (Eds.), *Machine scoring of essays: Truth and consequences* (pp. 28–37). Logan: Utah State University Press.

Ericsson, P. F., & Haswell, R. H. (Eds.), (2006). *Machine scoring of essays: Truth and consequences.* Logan: Utah State University Press.

Ericsson, P. F., & Haswell, R. H. (2006). Introduction. In P. F. Ericsson & R. H. Haswell (Eds.), *Machine scoring of essays: Truth and consequences* (pp. 1–7). Logan: Utah State University Press.

ETS. (2007). *The e-rater overview.* Retrieved January 15, 2007, from http://www.ets.org

———. (2008a). *GRE: Graduate Record Examination.* Retrieved December 28, 2008, from www.ets.org/gre

———. (2008b). *The TOEFL test: Test of English as a foreign language.* Retrieved August 11, 2008, from www.ets.org/toefl

———. (2008c). *TOEIC speaking and writing sample tests.* Princeton, NJ: Educational Testing Service.

Fairtest.org. (2007). How standardized testing damages education. Retrieved August 31, 2007, from www.fairtest.org/facts/howharm.htm

Ferris, D. (2002). *Treatment of error in second language student writing.* Ann Arbor: University of Michigan Press.

Ferris, D. R., & Hedgcock, J. (2005). *Teaching ESL composition: Purposes, process and practice* (2nd ed.). Mahwah, NJ: Lawrence Erlbaum.

Ferris, D., Brown, J., Collins, D., Liu, H., & Stine, M. (2009). *Teachers' practices in responding to student writing.* Paper presented at the 43rd Annual TESOL Convention and Exposition, Denver, CO.

Freeman, D. E., & Freeman, Y. S. (2004). *Essential linguistics: What you need to know to teach reading, ESL, spelling, phonics, grammar.* Portsmouth, NH: Heinemann.

Freire, P. (1985). *The politics of education: Culture, power, and liberation.* South Hadley, MA: Bergin & Garvey.

———. (1970/1993). *Pedagogy of the oppressed.* New York: Continuum (20th anniversary edition).

Gallagher, C. W. (2007). *Reclaiming assessment: A better alternative to the accountability agenda.* Portsmouth, NH: Heinemann.

Gardner, H. (2006). *Multiple intelligences: New horizons in theory and practice.* New York: Basic Books.

Gottlieb, M., Cranley, M. E., & Cammilleri, A. (2007). *Understanding the WIDA English proficiency standards: A resource guide.* Board of Regents of the University of Wisconsin. Retrieved July 28, 2009, from www.wida.us/standards/elp.aspx

Graves, D. H. (2002) *Testing is not teaching: What should count in education.* Portsmouth, NH: Heinemann.

Grimes, D. (2005). *Assessing automated assessment: Essay evaluation software in the classroom* [Electronic version]. Published with proceedings of Computers and Writing Conference, Stanford University, Palo Alto, CA. Retrieved July 16, 2007, from http://www.ics.uci.edu/~grimesd/

Hacker, D. (2003). *A writer's reference* (5th ed.). Boston: Bedford/St. Martin's.

Hairston, M. (1982). The winds of change: Thomas Kuhn and the revolution in the teaching of writing. *College Composition and Communication, 33*(1), 76–88.

Hamp-Lyons, L. (1991). Scoring procedures for ESL contexts. In L. Hamp-Lyons (Ed.), *Assessing second language writing in academic contexts* (pp. 241–278). Norwood, NJ: Multilingual Matters.

———. (1996). The challenges of second-language writing assessment. In E. M. White, W. D. Lutz, & S. Kamusikiri (Eds.), *Assessment of writing: Politics, policies, practices* (pp. 226–240). New York: Modern Language Association of America.

———. (2000). Social, professional, and individual responsibility in language testing. *System 28*, 579–591.

———. (2001). Fourth generation writing assessment. In T. Silva & P. K. Matsuda (Eds.), *On second language writing* (pp. 117–127). Mahwah, NJ: Lawrence Erlbaum.

———. (2002). The scope of writing assessment. *Assessing Writing, 8*, 5–16.

———. (2003). Writing teachers as assessors of writing. In B. Kroll (Ed.), *Exploring the dynamics of second language writing* (pp. 162–189). New York: Cambridge University Press.

———. (2005). What is writing? What is "scholastic aptitude"? What are the consequences? SAT I Writing—a trip down memory lane. *Assessing Writing, 10*, 151–156.

———. (2006). Feedback in portfolio-based writing courses. In K. Hyland & F. Hyland (Eds.), *Feedback in second language writing: Contexts and issues* (pp. 140–161). New York: Cambridge University Press.

Hamp-Lyons, L., & Kroll, B. (1996). Issues in ESL writing assessment: An overview. *College ESL, 6*(1), 52–72.

Harklau, L., Losey, K. M., & Siegal, M. (Eds.). (1999). *Generation 1.5 meets college composition: Issues in the teaching of writing to U.S.-educated learners of ESL*. Mahwah, NJ: Lawrence Erlbaum.

Harris, M. (1999*). Prentice Hall reference guide to grammar and usage* (4th ed.). Upper Saddle River, NJ: Prentice Hall.

Haswell, R. H. (1998). Searching for Kiyoko: Bettering mandatory ESL writing placement. *Journal of Second Language Writing, 7*, 133–174.

Haswell, R. H. (2002, October 11). Personal interview. West Lafayette, IN: Symposium on Second Language Writing.

———. (2005). Automated text-checkers: A chronology and a bibliography of commentary. *Computers and Composition Online: An International Journal*, 1–58. Retrieved October 12, 2006, from www.bgsu.edu/cconline/prodev.htm

———. (2006). Automatons and automated scoring: Drudges, black boxes, and dei ex machina. In P. F. Ericsson & R. Haswell (Eds.), *Machine scoring of essays: Truth and consequences* (pp. 57–78). Logan: Utah University Press.

Haswell, R., & Wyche-Smith, S. (1994). Adventuring into writing assessment. *College Composition and Communication, 45*, 220–236.

Hillocks, Jr., G. (2002). *The testing trap: How state writing assessments control learning*. New York: Teachers College Press.

Hirvela, A., & Sweetland, Y. L. (2005). Two case studies of L2 writers' experiences across learner-directed portfolio contexts. *Assessing Writing 10*, 192–213.

Hughes, A. (2003). *Testing for language teachers* (2nd ed.). Cambridge, UK: Cambridge University Press.

Huot, B. (1990). The literature of direct writing assessment: Major concerns and prevailing trends. *Review of Educational Research, 60*(2), 237–263.

———. (1994). A survey of college and university writing placement practices. *WPA: Writing Program Administration, 17*(3), 49–65.

———. (1996). Toward a new theory of writing assessment. *College Composition and Communication, 47*(4), 549–566.

———. (2001, March 15). Personal interview. Denver, CO: Conference on College Composition and Communication.

———. (2002). *(Re)Articulating writing assessment for teaching and learning.* Logan: Utah State University Press.

Inter American University of Puerto Rico, Ponce Campus. (2002). *Rubric to evaluate the primary traits of a composition.* Retrieved July 29, 2009, from www.ponce.inter.edu

Intersegmental Committee of the Academic Senates of the California Community Colleges, the California State University and the University of California. (2002). *Academic literacy: A statement of competencies expected of students entering California's public colleges and universities.* Retrieved February 11, 2004, from icas-ca.org/academic-literacy

Jacobs, H. L., Hartfiel, V. F., Hughey, J. B., & Wormuth, D. R. (1981). *Testing ESL Composition: A Practical Approach.* Boston: Newbury House.

Johnson, F. W. (1913). The Hillegas-Thorndike scale for measurement of quality in English composition. *The School Review, 1*(1), 39–49.

Johnson, K. E. (1999). *Understanding language teaching: Reasoning in action.* Boston: Heinle & Heinle.

Jones, E. (2006). ACCUPLACER's essay-scoring technology: When reliability does not equal validity. In P. F. Ericsson & R. Haswell (Eds.), *Machine scoring of essays: Truth and consequences* (pp. 93–113). Logan: Utah University Press.

Julian, E. (2005). Validity of the medical college admission test for predicting medical school performance. *Academic Medicine, 80*(10), 910–917.

Kaplan, R. B. (1966). Cultural thought patterns in intercultural education. *Language Learning, 16*, 1–20.

———. (2001). Foreword: What in the world is contrastive rhetoric? In C. G. Panetta (Ed.), *Contrastive rhetoric revisited and redefined* (pp. vii–xx). Mahwah, NJ: Lawrence Erlbaum.

Kasden, L. N., & Hoeber, D. R. (Eds.). (1980). *Basic writing: Essays for teachers, researchers, administrators*. Urbana, IL: National Council of Teachers of English.

Keith, T. Z. (2003). Validity of automated essay scoring systems. In M. D. Shermis & J. C. Burstein (Eds.), *Automated essay scoring: A cross-disciplinary perspective* (pp. 147–167). Mahwah, NJ: Lawrence Erlbaum.

Kohn, A. (2000). *The case against standardized testing: Raising the scores, ruining the schools*. Portsmouth, NH: Heinemann.

———. (2006). The trouble with rubrics. *English Journal, 95*(4), 12–15.

Kohn, A., & Shannon, P. (Eds.). (2002). *Education, Inc: Turning learning into business* (revised edition). Portsmouth, NH: Heinemann.

Krashen, S. D. (1987). *Principles and practice in second language acquisition*. Upper Saddle River, NJ: Prentice-Hall.

Kuhlman, N. (1999). The standards reform movement in the United States. *TESOL Matters, 9*(5). Retrieved May 4, 2007, from www.tesol.org/s_TESOL/sec_document.asp?CID=196&DID=821

Landauer, T. K., Laham, D., & Foltz, P. W. (1999). The intelligent essay assessor: Applications to educational technology. *Interactive Multimedia Electronic Journal of Computer-Enhanced Learning*. Wake Forest University. Retrieved October 12, 2007, from http://imej.wfu.edu/articles/1999/2/04/printver.asp

———. (2003). Automatic essay assessment. *Assessment in Education: Principles, Policy, & Practice, 10*(3), 295–308.

Lee, Y-W., Breland, H., & Muraki, E. (2004). Comparability of TOEFL CBT writing prompts for different native language groups. TOEFL Research Rep. No. RR-77, ETS RR-04-24). Princeton, NJ: ETS. Retrieved July 26, 2009, from www.ets.org/

Leki, I. (1992). *Understanding ESL writers: A guide for teachers*. Portsmouth, NH: Heinemann.

———. (1995). Good writing: I know it when I see it. In D. Belcher & G. Braine (Eds.), *Academic writing in a second language: Essays on research and pedagogy* (pp. 23–46). Norwood, NJ: Ablex.

Lewiecki-Wilson, C., Sommers, J., & Tassoni, J. P. (2000). Rhetoric and the writer's profile: Problematizing directed self-placement. *Assessing Writing, 7*, 165–183.

Li, X. (1995). *Good writing in cross-cultural context*. Albany: State University of New York Press.

Lindemann, E. (2001). *A rhetoric for writing teachers* (4th ed.). Oxford, UK: Oxford University Press.

Lips, D., & Feinberg, E. (2007). *The administrative burden of No Child Left Behind.* No. 1406. Published by The Heritage Foundation, Washington, DC. Retrieved February 20, 2009, from www.heritage.org/Research/Reports/2007/03/The_Administrative_Burden_of_No_Child_Left_Behind

Liu, J., & Hansen, J. G. (2002). *Peer response in second language writing classrooms.* Ann Arbor: University of Michigan Press.

Lynne, P. (2004). *Coming to terms: A theory of writing assessment.* Logan: Utah State University Press.

Mānoa Writing Program, University of Hawai i. (2009). *Benefits of peer review.* Retrieved July 26, 2009, from www.mwp.hawaii.edu/resources/peer_review.htm

Matsuda, P. K. (1997). Contrastive rhetoric in context: A dynamic model of L2 writing. *Journal of Second Language Writing, 6*(1), 45–60.

———. (2001). Reexamining audiolingualism: On the genesis of reading and writing in L2 studies. In D. Belcher & A. Hirvela (Eds), *Linking literacies: Perspectives on L2 reading-writing connections* (pp. 84–105). Ann Arbor: University of Michigan Press.

———. (2002). Alternative discourses: A synthesis. In C. Schroeder, H. Fox, & P. Bizzell (Eds.), *AltDis: Alternative discourses and the academy* (pp. 191–196). Portsmouth, NH: Boynton/Cook Heinemann.

———. (2003a). Process and post-process: A discursive history. *Journal of Second Language Writing, 12*, 65–83.

———. (2003b). Second language writing in the twentieth century: A situated historical perspective. In B. Kroll (Ed.), *Exploring the dynamics of second language writing* (pp. 15–34). New York: Cambridge University Press.

Matzen, R. N., & Sorensen, C. (2006). E-Write as a means for placement into three composition courses: A pilot study. In P. F. Ericsson & R. Haswell (Eds.), *Machine scoring of essays: Truth and consequences* (pp. 130–137). Logan: Utah University Press.

McAllister, K. S., & White, E. M. (2006). Interested complicities: The dialectic of computer-assisted writing assessment. In P. F. Ericsson & R. Haswell (Eds.), *Machine scoring of essays: Truth and consequences* (pp. 8–27). Logan: Utah University Press.

McGee, T. (2006). Taking a spin on the Intelligent Essay Assessor. In P. F. Ericsson & R. Haswell (Eds.), *Machine scoring of essays: Truth and consequences* (pp. 79–92). Logan: Utah University Press.

McNamara, T. (2000). *Language testing.* Oxford: Oxford University Press.

McNamara, T., & Roever, C. (2006). *Language testing: The social dimension.* Malden, MA: Blackwell.

McNeil, L. M. (2000). *Contradictions of school reform: Educational costs of standardized testing.* New York: Routledge.

Menken, K. (2005). *When the test is what counts: How high-stakes testing affects language policy and the education of English language learners in high school.* Retrieved May 15, 2009, from www.elladvocates.org/nclb/nclbstudies.html#diss

Messick, S. (1996). Validity and washback in language testing. *Language Testing, 13*(3) 241–256.

Metcalf, S. (2002). Reading between the lines. *The Nation*, 5/12/06. Retrieved May 21, 2006, from www.thenation.com/doc/20020128/metcalf

Miner, B. (2004–2005, Winter). Testing companies mine for gold. *Rethinking Schools,* p. 1.

Monroe, J. R. (2006). *Testing the low class: Standardized assessment in the lives of Hispanic ELL students.* Unpublished doctoral dissertation, University of Maryland, College Park. Retrieved May 19, 2009, from http://scholar.google.com/

Moravec, H. (1998). When will computer hardware match the human brain? *Journal of Evolution and Technology, 1*, 1–12. Retrieved November 24, 2007, from www.jetpress.org/volume1/moravec.htm

Murphy, S., & Grant, B. (1996). Portfolio approaches to assessment: Breakthrough or more of the same. In E. M. White, W. D. Lutz, & S. Kamusikiri, S. (Eds.). *Assessment of writing: Politics, policies, practices* (pp. 284–300) New York: Modern Language Association of America.

Murray, D. M. (1980). Writing as process: How writing finds its own meaning. In T. R. Donovan & B. W. McClelland (Eds.), *Eight approaches to teaching composition* (pp. 3–20). Urbana, IL: National Council of Teachers of English.

NCTE Executive Committee Writing Study Group. (2004). *NCTE beliefs about the teaching of writing.* Retrieved July 23, 2007, from www.ncte.org

Neill, M. (2005). *Assessment of ELL students under NCLB: Problems and solutions*. Retrieved May 19, 2009, from www.fairtest.org/files/NCLB_assessing_bilingual_students_0.pdf

Newkirk, T. (1994). The politics of intimacy: The defeat of Barrett Wendell at Harvard. In L. Tobin & T. Newkirk (Eds.), *Taking stock: The writing process movement in the 90's* (pp. 115–131). Portsmouth, NH: Boynton/Cook.

New Oriental Education and Technology Group. Retrieved March 8, 2008, from http://english.neworiental.org/Default.aspx?tabid=3463

New York State Education Department. (2009). *The teaching of language arts to limited English proficient/English language learners: Learning standards for English as a second language*. Albany, NY: The University of the State of New York, The State Education Department, Office of Bilingual Education.

Nichols, S. L., & Berliner, D. C. (2007). *Collateral damage: How high-stakes testing corrupts America's schools*. Cambridge, MA: Harvard University Press.

Ohanian, S. (1999). *One size fits few: The folly of educational standards*. Portsmouth, NH: Heinemann.

Ohio Department of Education. (2007). *Ohio English language proficiency standards for limited English proficient students*. Columbus: Ohio Department of Education.

O'Malley, J. M., & Valdez-Pierce, L. (1996). *Authentic assessment for English language learners: Practical approaches for teachers*. New York: Addison-Wesley.

O'Neill, P., Moore, C., & Huot, B. (2009). *A guide to college writing assessment*. Logan: Utah State University Press.

Orlich, D. C. (2007). *Poverty, ethnicity and high-stakes tests: A challenge for social and educational justice?* Paper presented at the Washington State Children's Justice Conference, Seattle, WA.

Orlich, D. C., & Gifford, G. (2007). Test scores, poverty, and ethnicity: The new American dilemma. *Washington State Kappan, 1*(1), pp. 32–37. Retrieved July 25, 2009, from www.pdkwa.org/

Page, E. B. (2003). Project essay grade: PEG. In M. D. Shermis & J. C. Burstein (Eds.), *Automated essay scoring: A cross-disciplinary perspective* (pp. 43–54). Mahwah, NJ: Lawrence Erlbaum.

Payan, R. M., & Nettles, M. T. (2008). *Current state of English language learners in the US K–2 student population*. Princeton, NJ: ETS.

Perelman, L. (2005, May). *New SAT: Write long, badly, and prosper.* Retrieved October 2, 2009, from http://articles.latimes.com/2005/may/29/opinion/oe-perelman29

Petruzzi, A. (2008). Articulating a hermeneutic theory of writing assessment. *Assessing Writing, 13*, 219–242.

Pontin, J. (2006). *Thinking machines: Danny Hillis talks about the real-world challenges of creating artificially intelligent machines.* Retrieved November 24, 2006, from www.technologyreview.com/printer_friendly_article.aspx?id=17709

Reid, J. M. (1993). *Teaching ESL writing.* Englewood Cliffs, NJ: Prentice Hall Regents.

Rice, L. (n.d.). SLATE Newsletter, National Council of Teachers of English. Retrieved August 11, 2008, from www.ncte.org

Rose, M. (1981). Sophisticated, ineffective books: The dismantling of process in composition texts. *College Composition and Communication, 32*, 65–74.

Ross, J. (1968). Controlled writing: A transformational approach. *TESOL Quarterly, 2*(4), 253–261.

Rothermel, B. A. (2006). Automated writing instruction: Computer-assisted or computer-driven pedagogies? In P. F. Ericsson & R. Haswell (Eds.), *Machine scoring of essays: Truth and consequences* (pp. 199–210). Logan: Utah University Press.

Royer, D. J., & Gilles, R. (1998). Directed self-placement: An attitude of orientation. *College Composition and Communication, 50*(1), 54–70.

Royer, D. J., & Gilles, R. (2003). (Eds.) *Directed self-placement: Principles and practices.* Cresskill, NJ: Hampton Press.

Rudner, L. M., Garcia, V., & Welch, C. (2006). An evaluation of the IntelliMetric™ essay scoring system. *Journal of Technology, Learning, and Assessment, 4*(4). Retrieved November 29, 2006, from www.jtla.org

Ruszkiewicz, J., Hairston, M., & Seward, D. E. (2001). *SF writer* (2nd ed.). New York: Longman.

Samway, K. D., & McKeon, D. (1999). *Myths and realities: Best practices for language minority students.* Portsmouth, NH: Heinemann.

Shannon, P. (1995). *text, lies & video tape: stories about life, literacy, and learning.* Portsmouth, NH: Heinemann.

———. (2001). *iSHOP you shop.* Portsmouth, NH: Heinemann.

———. (2007). *Reading against democracy: The broken promises of reading instruction*. Portsmouth, NH: Heinemann.

Shaughnessy, M. P. (1977). *Errors and expectations*. New York: Oxford University Press.

Shermis, M. D., & Burstein, J. C. (Eds.). (2003). *Automated essay scoring: A cross-disciplinary perspective*. Mahwah, NJ: Lawrence Erlbaum.

Shohamy, E. (2001). *The power of tests*. New York: Longman.

Shohamy, E., Donitsa-Schmidt, S., & Ferman, I. (1996). Test impact revisited: Washback effect over time. *Language Testing, 13*(3) 298–317.

Shor, I. (1992). *Empowering education: Critical teaching for social change*. Chicago: University of Chicago Press.

———. (1997). Our apartheid: Writing instruction & inequality. *Journal of Basic Writing, 16*(1), 91–104.

Silva, T. (1993). Toward an understanding of the distinct nature of L2 writing: The ESL research and its implications. *TESOL Quarterly, 27*(4), 657–675.

Silva, T., & Matsuda, P. K. (2002). Writing. In N. Schmitt (Ed.). *An introduction to applied linguistics* (pp. 251–266, 332–335). London: Arnold.

Smarthinking. (2008). *Online tutoring and writing services that help students succeed*. Retrieved March 30, 2008, from www.smarthinking.com

Soliday, M. (2002). *The politics of remediation: Institutional and student needs in higher education*. Pittsburgh: University of Pittsburgh Press.

Spandel, V. (2006). In defense of rubrics. *English Journal, 96*(1), 19–22.

Spolsky, B. (1978). Introduction: Linguists and language testers. In B. Spolsky (Ed.), *Approaches to language testing*. Washington, DC: Center for Applied Linguistics.

Stoynoff, S., & Chapelle, C. A. (2005). *ESOL tests and testing*. Alexandria, VA: Teachers of English to Speakers of Other Languages.

TESOL, Inc. (n.d.). *ESL Standards for Pre-K-12 Students, Online Edition*. Retrieved July 30, 2009, from www.tesol.org/s_tesol/seccss.asp?CID=113&DID=1583

Thorndike, E. L. (1913). Notes on the significance and use of the Hillegas scale for measuring the quality of English composition. *English Journal, 2*(9), 551–561.

Tremmel, M. (2003, September). The politics of teaching. SLATE Newsletter. Retrieved October 27, 2006, from www.ncte.org

University of the State of New York/New York State Education Department. (2009). *The teaching of language arts to limited English proficient/English language learners: Learning standards for English as a second language.* Retrieved July 27, 2009, from www.emsc.nysed.gov/biling/resource/ESL/standards.html

Valdez-Pierce, L. (2000, October 27). *Using assessment to inform instruction: Learning by doing.* Keynote presented at the Ohio TESOL Conference, Columbus, OH.

———. (2003). *Assessing English language learners.* Washington, DC: National Education Association.

Vantage Learning. (2005). *How IntelliMetric™ works.* Retrieved November 14, 2007, from www.vantagelearning.com/school/research/intellimetric.html

———. (2007). *MY Access! school edition: Because writing matters efficacy report.* Retrieved November 21, 2007, from www.vantagelearning.com/school/research/myaccess.html

Ware, P. (2006). Book Review. [Review of the book *The impact of new media on writing assessment]. Assessing Writing, 11*, 135–139.

Warschauer, M., & Grimes, D. (2008). Automated writing assessment in the classroom. *Pedagogies: An International Journal, 3*(1), 22–36.

Warschauer, M., & Ware, P. (2006). Automated writing evaluation: defining the classroom research agenda. *Language Teaching Research, 10*(2), 157–180.

Washington Post. (2006). Great moments in testing. Retrieved November 18, 2007, from www.washingtonpost.com

Weigle, S. C. (2002). *Assessing writing.* Cambridge, UK: Cambridge University Press.

———. (2007). Teaching writing teachers about assessment. *Journal of Second Language Writing, 16*, 194–209.

White, E. M. (1990). Language and reality in writing assessment. *College Composition and Communication, 41*(2), 187–200.

———. (1994). Issues and problems in writing assessment. *Assessing Writing, 1*, 11–27.

———. (1995). An apologia for the timed impromptu essay test. *College Composition and Communication, 46*(1), 30–45.

———. (1996a). Writing assessment beyond the classroom: Will writing teachers play a role? In L. Z. Bloom, D. A. Daiker, & E. M. White (Eds.), *Composition in the twenty-first century: Crisis and change* (pp. 101–111). Carbondale: Southern Illinois University Press.

———. (1996b). Power and agenda setting in writing assessment. In E. M. White, W. D. Lutz, & S. Kamusikiri, S. (Eds.). *Assessment of writing: Politics, policies, practices* (pp. 9–24). New York: Modern Language Association of America.

———. (1998). *Teaching and assessing writing: Understanding, evaluating and improving student performance.* San Francisco: Jossey-Bass.

———. (2001). The opening of the modern era of writing assessment: A narrative. *College English, 63*(3), 306–320.

———. (2003, August 25). Re: What is knowing comp theory/history good for? Retrieved August 26, 2003, from https://lists.asu.edu/cgi-bin/wa?A2-indo308&L-WPA-L&T-O&F-&5-&P-49204

———. (2007). *Assigning, responding, evaluating: A writing teacher's guide* (4th ed.). New York: Bedford/St. Martin's.

———. (2008). Testing in and testing out. *WPA: Writing Program Administration, 32*(1), 129–142.

White, E. M., Lutz, W. D., & Kamusikiri, S. (1996). *Assessment of writing: Politics, policies, practices.* New York: Modern Language Association of America.

Wilson, M. (2006). *Rethinking rubrics in writing assessment.* Portsmouth, NH: Heinemann.

Wolcott, W., & Legg, S. (1998). *An overview of writing assessment: Theory, research, and practice.* Urbana, IL: National Council of Teachers of English.

Yancey, K. B. (1999). Looking back as we look forward: Historicizing writing assessment. *College Composition and Communication, 50*(3), 483–503.

Zamel, V. (1982). Writing: The process of discovering meaning. *TESOL Quarterly, 16*(2), 195–209.

Zawilinski, L. (2009, May). HOT blogging: A framework for blogging to promote higher order thinking. *The Reading Teacher, 62*(8), 650–661.

Index

Page numbers followed by t indicate table

ACT, 121–122, 146, 168t, 176–177
analytic rubrics, 44
artificial intelligence, 166–167, 168t
assessment: characteristics, 14–17, 33, 80; control of, vii, 5–6, 10–13, 72–73, 129–131, 185; criteria, 70–72, 102–104; design, 33–50; history, 19–27; political aspects, 110–112, 129–131; purposes, 5–6, 8–9, 32; responsibility for, vii, 2–3, 9–13, 159–160, 177–179, 185; training needed, 181–182; types, 14, 56–57, 77–85, 108–109, 128, 132, 176; views on, vii, 14–17. *See also* biases; tests, standardized
assignments: bias in, 87–88; compare and contrast, 64, 65–67; design of, 59–64, 68–70, 72–73; essays, 64, 68–69, 70, 74–76; in-class writing, 71; peer review, 77–78, 104–107; reflection letter, 47–48; shaped by assessment, 101–104. *See also* curriculum
asynchronous communication, 138–141
automated essay scoring. *See* machine scoring

biases: contrastive rhetoric and, 105–107; definition, 86; development of, 88; of grammar errors, 98–101; of L2 students, 97–98; in peer review, 104–107; personality type and, 91–92; political, 111–113; in tests, 87–88, 107–111, 125–126
Blake, R.J., 138–142
Bloch, J., 138–140, 142–143
blogs, 140–141
Breland, H., 87, 158
Broad, B., 12, 16, 19, 26, 43, 158
Brown, H.D., 33, 45, 46, 72, 87–88, 128
Burstein, J.C., 157, 159, 161–162, 164, 173, 177, 179

California Intersegmental Committee, 89–90
chat rooms, 142, 153–154
Chodorow, M., 157, 177
College Board, 120–121, 126–127, 167, 168t
COMPASS, 107, 168t
computer-mediated communication (CMC), 138–139, 142
computer-mediated discourse (CMD), 138–139, 142
Connor, U., 105–106
consequential validity, 41
construct validity, 41
content standards, 34–35
content validity, 41
contrastive rhetoric, 105–107
Cornett, C., 102–104
costs, testing, 115–116
course catalog descriptions, 62–63
criteria development, 70–72
CRITERION, 158, 168t, 174

criterion validity, 41
Crusan, D., 2, 12–13, 29, 73, 93–94, 96, 102–104, 107–109, 111, 144–145, 153, 175, 181
cultural capital, 59, 134
curriculum: assessment design and, 33–50; assessment impact on, 10–13; assignment design and, 59–64, 68–70, 72–73; influence of standardized testing on, 127–128; maintaining control of, 72–73; NCLB impacts, 42–43, 131–132

deficit theory, 23–24
Delpit, L.D., 59, 134
descriptors, 60–61
direct assessment, 108
discussion, online, 138–143

EduMetry, 149–150
Elluminate®, 138, 142
email, 139–140
Emig, J., 24, 92
English as a Second Language. *See* second language teaching
e-rater, 124, 164–165, 168t, 177
Educational Records Privacy Act (ERPA), 139–140
ESL. *See* second language teaching
essays: process, 70; in testing, 20, 26–27, 126–129; timed, 64, 68–69, 126–128; writing prompts, 68–69, 71, 87–88. *See also* machine scoring
ETS, 116–119, 122–124, 158–159, 164–165, 168t
e-Write, 176–177

face validity, 41
Ferris, D.R., 46, 59, 72, 91, 98, 101, 153, 181
formative assessments, 56–57
Freire, P., 130–131

Generation 1.5 students, 119–122
goals, 62–63
grammar and bias, 98–101
GRE, 122–124

Hamp-Lyons, L., 2, 4, 6, 9–10, 12, 14, 16, 18–20, 27, 30, 46, 108–109, 127–128, 153, 174–175, 180
Hansen, J.G., 77, 104–105
Haswell, R.H., 7, 11–12, 50, 108–109, 126, 161, 163, 164, 172, 175, 178–179
Hedgcock, J., 46, 59, 72, 101
holistic rubrics, 44, 45–46
Huot, B., 1, 7, 12, 16–19, 28, 32, 80, 107–108, 145, 153, 175, 185

in-class writing assignments, 71
indirect assessment, 14, 108
Intelligent Essay Assessor (IEA), 165–166, 168t, 171–172
IntelliMetric ®, 166–167, 168t, 172
Internet: paper mills, 146–148; TOEFL testing, 116–118

Kaplan, R.B., 105–106
Knowledge Analysis Technologies, 165

language: acquisition process, 91, 99, 182; proficiency tests, 116–119; testing theories, 27–30
large-scale assessment. *See* tests, standardized
latent semantic analysis (LSA), 165–166, 168t
Leki, I., 8, 64, 96, 171
Liu, J., 77, 104–105, 181
low English proficiency (LEP) writing, 34–37

machine scoring: ability to read for meaning, 171–172; accountability in, 183–184; advantages, 172–173; debate about, 156–157; definition, 157; disadvantages, 173–174; effects of, 170; evolution of, 161–164; how it works, 160; and L2 students, 176–177; products, 164–170; professional opinions on, 174–175; student benefits, 158–159

Matsuda, P.K., 17, 29, 93, 96, 171
Matzen, R.N., 176–177
McAllister, K.S., 157, 161
McNamara, T., 33–34, 108, 185
Menken, K., 132, 133
multiple-trait rubrics, 46
MY Access! ®, 167, 168t, 169–170, 173, 174, 176

natural language processing (NLP), 164–165, 168t
NCLB. *See* No Child Left Behind (NCLB)
New York standards, 35–36
NLP (natural language processing), 164–167, 168t
No Child Left Behind (NCLB): costs, 115; criticism, 126, 130; effects, 42–43, 110; and L2 students, 131–133; and Obama administration, 133; standardized testing and, 110
norm referencing, 132

Obama administration, 133
objectives, 38–39
objectivity in testing, 124–126
ODSP (online directed self-placement), 144–146
Ohio standards, 34–35, 37
online directed self-placement (ODSP), 144–146
online discussion, 137–142

Pearson Knowledge Technologies, 165–166, 168t
peer review, 77–78, 104–107
PEG (Project Essay Grader), 163
performance standards, 35
personality and biases, 91–92
placement, student, 107–111, 126, 144–146
plagiarism, 147–149
political bias, 111–113
portfolio assessment, 27, 79–80
practicality, 42
primary trait rubrics, 44, 46
process essay, 70
progress indicators, 61–62, 64
Project Essay Grader (PEG), 161
prompts, writing, 68–69, 71, 87–88

real-time communication, 142–143, 153 183
reliability, 16–17, 39–40, 124–126
Roever, C., 33–34, 185
Rose, M., 24–25
rubrics: about, 43–44, 50; assessment goals and, 72–73; assignments and, 44; development of, 44, 73; examples, 45, 48–49, 51–54, 74–76, 81–84; negative views of, 43–44; sources for, 72; types of, 44–46

SAT®, 119–121, 126–129, 146
second language teaching: about good writing, 97–98; assignment development, 64–69; communicative competence, 171; course development, 59–63; criteria development, 70–72; NCLB impacts, 131–133; preparing for standardized tests, 133–136; rubric use, 44–46; standards, 34–37, 60–62; training needs, 181–182; writing for different fields, 94–95. *See also* students; teachers and teaching
Silva, T., 29, 171
SMARTHINKING ®, 150–152
Sorensen, C., 176–177
Spolsky, B., 27, 29
standards, 34–37, 60–62
students: assessment criteria development, 33, 44, 72, 102–104; biases of, 104–107; cultural capital and, 59, 133; Generation 1.5, 119–122; Internet paper mills use, 146–148; language

acquisition, 90, 98, 182; machine scoring and, 158–159, 176–177; NCLB effects on, 131–133; online communication tools, 133–143; peer review and, 77–78, 104–107; placement of, 107–111, 126, 145–146; standardized tests and, 107–111, 115–123, 133–136; statistics on, 180–181
Students Will Be Able To (SWBAT), 38–39, 62
StyleWriter, 152
summative assessments, 56–57
Swain, M., 171
SWBAT (Students Will Be Able To), 38–39, 62
synchronous communication, 138–139, 142–143

teachers and teaching: assessment preferences, 92–94; assessment responsibilities, 2–3, 9–13, 159–160, 177–179, 185; biases, 88–95, 98–102; control of assessment process, 5–6, 10–13, 17–19, 129–131, 185; de-skilling, 151, 153, 170; inconsistency in assessment, 96, 98; literacy expectations, 89–90; machine scoring use, 148–154, 177–179; personal experiences in assessment, 58–59; reasons not to assess, vii, 10–11; technology and, 137–138, 182–184; training needs, 181–182. *See also* second language teaching
technology: assessment and, 138–148; effects on teaching, 137–138, 148–154, 182–186; and L2 students, 142–143; online communication tools, 138–143; online tutoring, 153–154; self-placement assessments, 144–146. *See also* machine scoring; tests, standardized
TESOL, 36, 38, 53–54, 60–61
testing: bias in, 87–88; costs, 115–116; history of, 20–23; practicality, 42; reliability, 16–17, 39–40, 124–126; validity, 17, 41–42, 124–126; washback, 42–43. *See also* tests, standardized
tests, standardized: accountability in, 184–185; admission tests, 119–124, 129; advantages, 124–126; bias in, 107–111; business of, 115–116, 124; disadvantages, 126–129; history of 20–23, 25–27; impact on assessment, 6–7; language proficiency tests, 116–119; and parental income, 126; political bias and, 111–113; preparing students, 133–136; used for placement, 125; written essays in, 126–129. *See also* testing
TOEFL ®, 116–118, 178
TOEIC ®, 118–119
tutoring, online, 153–154
TWE (Test of Written English), 118–119

Valdez-Pierce, L., 33–35, 72, 101, 132
validity, 17, 41–42, 124–126
Vantage Learning, 166–167, 168t, 169–170, 171–172

Ware, P., 156, 161, 163, 170–171, 177–178
Warschauer, M., 156, 161, 163, 177–178
washback, 42–43
Weigle, S.C., 1, 9, 10, 12, 16, 18, 72, 117, 136, 143, 175, 177, 181
White, E.M., 1, 11, 12, 15, 17–19, 26–28, 69, 79, 89, 109, 128–129, 145, 153, 157–158, 161, 175, 185
wikis, 141
World-Class Instructional Design and Assessment (WIDA), 36

WritePlacer, 167, 168t
WriteToLearn, 160, 168t
writing: ability definitions, 7–8, 13–14; academic preferences in, 93–95; definition of good, 93, 96–98, 131; differing views on, 13–14; meaning in, plagiarism, 147–149; process of, 9, 24–25, 92; prompts, 68–69, 71, 87–88; standards, 34–37; teacher training needed, 181–182; technology impacts, 143–148. *See also* assignments
Wysche-Smith, S., 11, 50

Yancey, K.B., 10–12, 14, 16–17, 19–20